CANYON

CANYON

Books by John van der Zee

THE PLUM EXPLOSION

BLOOD BROTHERHOOD

LIFE IN THE PEACE ZONE
(*with Hugh Wilkerson*)

ON

The Story of the Last Rustic Community
in Metropolitan America

John van der Zee

279514

Harcourt Brace Jovanovich, Inc.
New York

The photographs are used by the kind permission
of the Oakland, California, *Tribune*.

This book is dedicated to
EARL SHORRIS

AUTHOR'S NOTE

For materials used in the preparation of this book
I am indebted to Brother Lewis Dennis Goodman, FSC,
Assistant Librarian of St. Mary's College;
to Tony Biggs, of the Oakland Tribune;
and to Tay Sloan, Doug McMillan, and Bruce Baillie.

Contents

Contents

Illustrations

Between pages 78 and 79

Redwood grove, Canyon, California

Not giant soccer balls, but a characteristic Canyon house,
consisting of three geodesic domes joined together

Inside a geodesic-dome house

County notices: Officialdom posts a warning
on the tumble-down store and post office

Fait accompli: If people are still getting mail there,
how can the county deny a permit for its reconstruction?

Resistance, 1967: Canyon residents, defying the county,
join forces to rebuild without permits

Canyon store and post office as reconstructed by volunteer labor

Canyon store and post office two years later,
the morning after the gasoline-pipeline break and the holocaust

xiii

What you need in this situation is a sewer system that's sure-fire, like Apollo Eleven. You need a system that will get you to the moon and back.

—Managing Engineer, East Bay
Municipal Utilities District,
before the Contra Costa County
(California) Board of Supervisors,
August, 1969

Part One

One / Roust

On the morning of February 17, 1969, a force of ten helmeted sheriff's deputies, three county building inspectors, two agents of the California State Narcotics Bureau, and a dogcatcher with a tranquilizer-shooting rifle swept into the small, rustic Northern California community of Canyon, just over the hills from Berkeley and across the Bay from San Francisco, and posted notices ordering forty people, nearly a quarter of the community's residents, to vacate their houses—houses that they had built themselves, in most cases on their own land.

What took place in Canyon on February 17 was an episode in a much larger drama, a story that has, as yet, no ending. And whose beginning lies in some dusty corner of that mental attic we call The West.

On that day in Canyon, the inspectors and guards rode into the community on a wide, level path—the former roadbed of the Sacramento-Northern Railway. Leaving their official vehicles, they followed one of the inspectors along damp forest pathways known only to the inspector and the people he was about to evict, walked to a series of odd-looking houses—a metal

3

materials shed, a barn, a tree house, a huge beam-and-timber skeleton, a house made mostly of old windows—and stapled to each dwelling a DO NOT ENTER notice, declaring it unsafe, allowing the occupants forty-eight hours to vacate, and threatening them with a $500 fine or six months' imprisonment if the notice was disobeyed. There was a furtive, outlaw quality about this part of Canyon—its shady walkways, its plasmic shapelessness, its architectural radicalism—that seemed to suggest that life here was like photographic film, protected by darkness and vulnerable to exposure; and though there was some argument and discussion and picture taking on the part of the occupants of the posted houses, there was nothing that looked like organized resistance.

It was only afterward, when the officers had withdrawn from the steep, unfamiliar woods, climbed back into their cars, and driven up a paved, winding road past more conventional houses and into the sunlight near the top of a ridge, to where the police could have been expected to proceed without irritating physical exertion, that the attitude of the people of the community suddenly seemed to change. Now, 400 feet above the highway, where the pavement ended and the trees thinned a little and you could look out over the whole hillside and see where you were, the road was blocked by an enormous barricade of six-by-six beams, with the skull of a cow set on top and an old green pickup truck parked on the other side. Out in the open, in sunlight, at a narrow spot in the road, a crowd of people was watching, with cameras and a television crew, as though collecting evidence.

The county-painted trucks and station wagons stopped, one behind the other in a tight file before the barricade, and the officers inside climbed out. As they did, another line of vehicles climbed up the road behind them—old junky cars, pickups, jeeps, stuffed with people hanging from running boards and leaning out windows. They were honking horns and yelling and singing. More people were coming out on foot from behind the barricade and up and down from both sides of the road. Most of them were young and hairy, and there were big dogs with them, trotting around and barking. Everyone was smiling as if it was all in fun, and there seemed to be no point in making a show of force. But they had the officers cut off on both sides.

As they stood staring at the crowd and at the enormous pile of beams, it began to dawn on the officers that a community mind had been at work down below and up here since the time they had first driven onto the old roadbed, a mind that combined an intelligent grasp of confrontation tactics with a shrewd sense of publicity, and had reversed the current of the day's proceedings. Looking out over the hillside, the officers saw that that mind had chosen the perfect spot to make a stand.

Below, through a long ravine overflowing with evergreens, a creek winds among cool, dark redwood flats; above the creek, the land sweeps upward in a slope, where smaller redwoods are mixed with bay trees and madrone, and you can see, here and there among the trees, the peaked, chimneyed roofs of old summer cottages. Off to the right and climbing is the straight community, a long curve of narrow, bumpy, community-paved road with modest, well-kept rustic houses to either side, with gardens and porches and wooden steps, the houses scattering as the road approaches the top of the ridge, the trees fading into grasslands and the sun getting warmer, and the pavement ending at a crossroad, where you stare out over land so angular you look *down* at hawks circling over the tops of redwood trees.

It was like being in a park here, or standing on one of the back-country trails of the Sierras; there was the same sense of air and space and profound meaning in subtle movement that cuts through all the layers of civilized behavior and—under other circumstances—might make you want to strip naked or yell or lie on the ground and watch the foliage of the trees rushing across the sky. It was that feeling, that urge to return to a simpler, more innocent existence, that seemed now to be magnified into something frightening by the crowd: the long-haired, bearded, or mustached men in their patched, faded Levis, work shirts, woolly lumbermen's jackets, boots; the girls, long-haired, some in their teens, several pregnant, a few in long, loose, short-waisted gowns.

The officers stood staring at the barricade. They weren't about to start trying to take it apart; yet beyond, according to the building inspectors, were more violations: illegal shacks and domes and suspension walks, plastic water pipe, and bootlegged jump-line electricity. They'd have to leave the cars here and continue on foot, or else back all the cars down the hill with everybody watching, only to have to come all the way out here again another time. For a moment, it seemed as if nothing was going to happen. Then the sheriff's sergeant started walking toward the pile of beams.

"Stop!"

He stopped. A tall young man with a black mustache and dangling black hair that he had to keep brushing out of his eyes was yelling at them from the high side of the road, striding along the rank of officers, scolding them in front of the crowd.

"We do not give you permission to be on our property. You are trespassing. We will not obstruct you in any way, but you are trespassing."

The sergeant searched the watching faces, and found them without sympathy. No dumb hippies, these, invoking the law against The Law. His officers could lose control of the situation if they didn't assert themselves. His eyes returned to the young man with the dangling hair, on whom he fixed a stern, official stare.

"What's your name?" he demanded.

The man gave his name and added, "And what is your name, sir?"

Flustered, the sergeant muttered his name and rank. People were pointing cameras at him. His men looked embarrassed. He had led them into a public-relations ambush, and they were within inches of slipping into the role of authoritarian thugs. It was no place to hold a debate or start making arrests. Instead, trying to rise above the situation before the hostile eyes of the cameras and the crowd, the sergeant quietly directed his men around the barricade. The men were still uneasy. The narcotics agents were grinning at the crowd, trying to be Good Guys. Only the inspector from the Housing Authority, picking his way carefully around the beams, looked oblivious to what was going on among the people watching.

Alone among the officers, he walked on familiar ground. A dedicated and curious man, the inspector had walked these paths before, wearing a rainhat and green anticontamination coveralls, trudging up and down steep dirt steps, circling around large trees, mincing downhill in the slick rain-forest gloom to examine the strange, cleverly constructed places where these even stranger people chose to live, jotting down violations in his note pad. Sometimes, in his legal capacity as a Housing Authority officer, he inspected a homesite while the residents were there, being careful to ask their permission to do so. At other times, expanding his authority (asserting initiative, one might say), he entered upon and examined private lands when no one else was present. If the occupants came home while he was there, he gave them one of his business cards, smiled, and left. If they didn't come home, he often collected evidence in the form of Polaroid photographs, not only of building-code violations but of health and sanitation offenses, too. Once, he had photographed some marijuana drying inside one of these houses, and on the strength of his photographs a warrant had been issued for the occupant's arrest. The evidence hadn't held up in court, but the young man who had been arrested was outraged. "I'll kill you!" he had screamed at the inspector. So this time the inspector had come accompanied by an armed escort and narcotics men, just in case.

There had been other evidence against the community, in particular a tape recording made by the son of one of the older residents, a tape of a screeching rock band that a boy known as

SuperJoel had invited out to Canyon one weekend afternoon.

"The band came up and started setting up at the top of the hill," says a young man who was living just a few yards away. "I didn't want to tell them not to, though I hated the idea and their music. After about an hour, the cops came out. They refused to do anything. Grant Marks [the son of one of the older residents, recently discharged from the Air Police] was furious. Finally the cops left. SuperJoel started yelling insults into the microphone, and Grant tape-recorded it:

FUCK MRS. SO-AND-SO!
MRS. MARKS IS A BITCH!

"Grant played the tape for the President of the Board of Supervisors. That was wrong. Grant doesn't live in Canyon. He should have punched SuperJoel in the mouth instead of going outside."

Now the building inspector led the officers past a bizarre-looking house, half-open, roofed with eucalyptus poles, and up a rutted fire trail to the crown of the ridge, from which you can see for miles.

Off to the right was the wide slope of Redwood Regional Park, a refreshing green wall of spruce, pine, redwood, and fir, stretching beyond view east and west. To the left was a small valley, where cattle browsed in thick grass, brown most of the year, but green now from heavy February rains. Immediately around the fire trail were smaller trees, live oak and knobcone pine. It was as unlikely a setting as there probably has ever been for a mass eviction.

The February sun was hot in the open, and the trail had been steep. The deputies were sweating beneath their helmets, and the brush whipped their clothes as the inspector led them off the fire trail and along more winding paths to strange, elaborately conceived houses that appeared with startling abruptness among the trees and brush. The people, some of them barefoot, followed; and the dogs. Things were a little friendlier now.

8

Longhairs chatted with the officers, some of whom even expressed admiration for the effort and ingenuity that had gone into the houses that they were posting. There was a large, hive-like structure, a latticework of curved and fastened plywood in the shape of three joined domes, that exposed as much as it sheltered and looked as if it had grown organically out of the soil. At the bottom of a steep, rough trail, another dome, larger and more elaborate than the first, rested on a wide deck with a spectacular view of the redwoods. It could have been worth between $30,000 and $40,000, yet there was a Tobacco Road pen of chickens outside and a dozen puppies tumbling around and a row of Levis-wearing longhairs sitting, feet dangling, on the deck.

When the Housing Authority inspector had finished posting this last house, the man who had built it—the same young man with long hair who had confronted the officers at the top of the road—offered to show him a short cut down the hillside, and he led the officers along the line of the ridge and down the slope to the bottom of the hill to where the community schoolhouse is. The official party walked and walked, sweating, slapped by branches, breathing dust. About a third of the way down, the inspector complained that he thought the young man had been deceptive, and the young man replied that he thought the same of the inspector. When the officers reached the end of the trail, rumpled, dirty, and exhausted, they realized that they were out of the community. No matter; the job was done.

The situation that had arisen in Canyon rested, at bottom, on an absurdity: that what was wrong about building a house in Canyon was also what was right about building a house in Canyon.

Tucked away on one side of an isolated ravine within a mile of the city limits of Oakland and less than fifteen miles from San Francisco, the tiny 120-year-old community of Canyon is surrounded by park and watershed lands of the regional water company, the East Bay Municipal Utilities District. By fencing off these lands and sequestering them as a water source while other county communities grew into suburban towns, the utilities district, whose name is MUD in Canyon, has kept that corner of the county a green belt, out of the lock-step march of two-car garages and family rooms over the county's remaining orchards and hills.

At the same time, fearing contamination of its Upper San Leandro Reservoir, into which the creek below the community flows, East Bay MUD in 1951 adopted a policy of buying up and tearing down whatever homes became available in the area bordering their fenced-off, unpopulated park and watershed. In Canyon, this rustic redevelopment policy, zealously pursued during the 1950's and 1960's, restored natural vegetation, brought about an upsurge in wildlife, increased privacy—and reduced the community by half its homes and more than half its people. Canyon's fortune, its location, was also Canyon's flaw.

Between 1940 and 1965, while nearby suburban towns doubled and tripled in size, the population of Canyon shrank from nearly 400 to about 130, and the number of homes, mostly old summer houses, from eighty to forty. Residents grew old; some died, while others merely tired of the discomfort that is part of life in a rustic community and moved away. In the 1950's, the Canyon Store lost its permit to sell produce, the Canyon Dance Hall quit bringing newcomers out, and there were periodic rumors that the post office would be shut down. By the early 1960's, with enrollment in the Canyon School threatening to drop below the state-required minimum for the first time since 1918, Canyon was like a lone rustic outpost in a wilderness of urban growth, without a sidewalk, a sewer, a street light, or a public official.

It wasn't that there weren't any young people interested in moving to Canyon. It was just that the risks involved in doing so were, to them, too great.

If you wanted to buy a house in Canyon, you had to pay cash, full price. Because of the possibility of condemnation or fire, banks wouldn't finance loans on Canyon property, nor would casualty companies underwrite fire insurance. The few old summer houses occasionally available lacked a sewer system, had a rationed supply of water, and were often in disrepair. If your fancy for living close to nature overcame these disadvantages, and you had $8,000 to $16,000 in cash ready to invest in an uninsured forty-year-old house, you still had to meet or top the bid of East Bay MUD, which was willing to make a cash offer on any house that was for sale. Not surprisingly, among the houses already bought and demolished by 1965 were the most substantial (and expensive) in Canyon.

While Canyon was quietly disappearing house by house, just over the hills in Berkeley a metaphysical rebellion was beginning, a fresh testing of society's limits that, provoking official reaction, led to spectacles of conflict—free speech, civil rights, antiwar—which inevitably intensified both the individual sense of oppression and the longing to return to a natural community.

Again and again, among the young people of Berkeley in the mid-1960's, there occurred the awareness described by Albert Camus in The Rebel: "the sudden, dazzling perception that there is something in man with which he can identify himself, if only for a moment."

Among this new generation of rebels, with their sense of infringed-upon rights and new-found loyalty to certain aspects of themselves, were some who discovered in nearby, yet nearly unknown Canyon the natural community with which they could identify themselves and demand respect. Individually, or by word of mouth, through visits to friends or solitary wanderings along the backroads near Berkeley, they found in this redwood retreat, with its isolation, its closeness to nature, its marginal housing, and its sense of a functioning yet unstructured community, a place to say "no" to society while saying "yes" to life. Alone or together, they were willing to put up money, bid against the utilities district, sink their savings in uncomfortable old houses or build new ones, challenge the county ordinances, and even go to jail if necessary in order to make one last desperate stand in behalf of their individual integrity.

The fact that this refusal "to let society touch what one is" included an indulgence in long hair, drugs, untidiness, and unorthodox living relationships was to make them enemies in the existing community almost immediately. And it helped lead to the present irony: those most responsible for revitalizing the community were about to be evicted from it.

The evening following the postings, most of the people of Canyon assembled in one of the two rooms of the Canyon School, their feelings of moral certitude confirmed by the day's spectacle of their community as victim.

Not only the young people were present; a few of the older residents, drawn by bonds of sympathy or community loyalty, had come to offer assistance and advice.

Although they had been aware that the inspectors were coming and had spent two days cleaning and picking up, the people whose houses had been posted were stunned and indignant at what they felt was a revelation of the true official resentment against them. After all, guns? Cops? Narcs? A dogcatcher? The President of the Board of Supervisors, who had pressed hardest for the postings, had intimated earlier to people from the community that he would wait until a legal appeal had been made, and had promised to come out to Canyon and investigate conditions for himself. He had done neither. And the enforcement of the county building code had been arbitrary and capricious. One man's otherwise legal home had been condemned for lacking off-road parking for two cars. "I'm not even on a street!" he protested. A child's tree house had been cited for not having room separations, hot and cold running water, a shower or bathtub, and a flush toilet. A dome house, condemned for being without sewerage facilities, lay beyond the legal boundaries where such facilities are required. There was angry talk of armed resistance,

and photographs of the Negro narcotics men had been sent to the newspaper of the Black Panther Party.

Cooler, more deliberate steps were also being taken. Doug Page, an attorney and former mayor of the town of Walnut Creek, had agreed to represent the posted homeowners and had already obtained a temporary restraining order against the county's action. It was agreed that suit would be filed for damages on behalf of the families involved. And formal planning was under way for a proposed Canyon Special Services District, which would give the community its own self-supported sewer, water, fire protection, and garbage system, ease the utilities district's fears of contamination, allow the posted houses to conform to the county building code, and get the community neck once and for all off the official block. Maybe.

Two / Slash

As bad as things might become in Canyon, there had been a time when they were far worse—when this pleasant, wooded pocket was as physically degraded as Lake Erie or industrial New Jersey. The countryside had been ravaged until men would not live in it. And yet it had come back.

Once, this ravine and the steep hills around it had been called simply The Redwoods: a nearly pure stand of Pacific Coast *Sequoia sempervirens* that included trees of enormous height and width. The Spanish land-grant tract in which Canyon lies, Laguna de los Palos Colorados (Lake of the Red Trees), is named for them, and the surrounding five-square-mile tract of slopes, benches, and flats was known for decades as the San Antonio Redwoods. Here, just east of and over the hills from San Francisco Bay, sheltered from wind, with rich alluvial soil and abundant moisture, is one of the farthest points inland that the coastal redwoods have ever grown. Unlike the great belt of redwoods along California's far-northern coast, this isolated group of trees was also exposed to the warm temperatures and long sunlight of the interior valleys, which produced a freakish grove of giants that probably surpassed in height anything now standing.

A British naval officer wrote in his journal in 1826 that trees growing on these slopes were conspicuous points of navigation, which could be used from the entrance of San Francisco Bay, sixteen miles away. And surviving stumps, which people came to gawk at long after the trees were gone, have been measured at up to twenty-one feet in diameter, not counting bark.

Probably the first trees were felled by the Spanish as far back as 1800, and it is known that The Redwoods supplied the main timbers for the permanent buildings of Mission San Jose, about thirty miles to the south.

For a long time the very size of the trees discouraged large-scale attempts to cut them. After all, even after you had done the week-long work of preparing a bed and whipsawing down one of these giants, you still had only a 70- to 200-ton raw log, miles from a settlement or even a mill. It was rugged country to haul timber in commercially, and more accessible redwoods were being cut by the Mexicans to the south and by the Russians to the north. By 1842, when John Sutter had opened mills in the Sierras and logging was going full-scale near Santa Cruz, the demand for San Antonio redwood had all but ceased.

Four years later, though, the first of a new breed of men began trickling into The Redwoods. These were American immigrants, unbound by the restrictions of a social or religious hierarchy, willing and able to subdue the wilderness through sheer physical effort and determined to become rich and powerful. Many of them would become respected local and state figures, but now they were men on the make, dodging soldiers of the Mexican alcalde and poaching timber from other men's land with a talent for exploitation unseen in this country before. One American, in one summer month in 1847, made 15,000 shingles from one tree. And in 1849 Harry Meiggs, a San Francisco lumberman, sent an army of loggers and disillusioned miners into The Redwoods and made a half-million dollars on the wood they brought out.

There were towns going up around the Bay now—San Francisco, Martinez, Benicia—booming thanks to the Gold Rush; and the towns needed wood. Over the hills from The Redwoods the lumber port of San Antonio sprang up, eventually to become the city of Oakland.

Yet so dense were the trees and so high was their lumber yield that even this stepped-up logging left the grove essentially undamaged. Sailors were still using The Redwoods as a navigational reference.

Then, early in 1850, the first steam sawmills began operating in the East Bay redwood forest. It was the end of the era of the saw pit, the split wedge, and the black-powder blasting of trees into workable sections, and the beginning of the end for the redwoods. A group of timber operators, many of whom had obtained lands by fraudulence or claim jumping, set busily to work, trying to outrace one another in mining out the forest, which they assumed would never grow again. As builders discovered the fire-and-insect-resistant qualities of redwood lumber, and lumber shipments from the East declined, the price of local lumber rose, intensifying logging activity. The mills became the economic center of the East Bay, and nearly all east-west roads were planned in relation to them. Teams of mules and oxen moved in heavy lumber traffic along what are now the county's main roads, and new routes opened as new towns inland sought access to the lumber they needed. Election returns from the time show a larger population in The Redwoods than anywhere else in the adjoining two counties.

The forest was now rapidly depleted. By 1854 the largest timber was becoming scarce; by 1857 there was no election precinct in The Redwoods; by 1860 all the mills had closed and most of the lands had been sold or simply abandoned. Not a single original redwood was left standing. All was stumps and waste; the flats and slopes had become the debris-strewn tracts that lumbermen call slash.

Most of the mill owners went on to become county supervisors, state legislators, or prominent businessmen, while the lumberjacks and millhands, the "notorious mob element from the redwoods," drifted elsewhere. Just recently a couple of the newer residents of Canyon ran across a picture from that time in a nearby college library. It was a group photograph of those long-ago loggers, with droopy mustaches, sideburns, unkempt beards, big hats, suspenders, boots.

"Hey," one Canyon newcomer said to the other. "They look like us!"

You can see the huge wheellike sections displayed in state parks and national forests from Southern Oregon south to San Luis Obispo, the rings marking the decades and the centuries in years of rain and drought and days of fire and storm. Sometimes the rings are marked with pins or arrows representing the signing of the Magna Carta, Columbus's landing, or Waterloo. But it is not until you realize that the rings of one redwood may represent the death of one tree and the growth from its roots of another that you begin to get some idea of the time these trees have been on the earth. And eventually you begin to wonder if they are part of our history or if we are part of theirs.

The coastal redwood, *Sequoia sempervirens*, is nearly as fantastic a tree below ground as it is above, with a broad, shallow root system whose regenerative power is so great that a single stump can nurse up to 500 new trees, or "suckers," some of which, given enough water and sunlight, will reach a height of eighty feet within thirty years. Because of this second growth, combined with the tendency of redwood seedlings to sprout in exposed mineral soil, new shoots had begun to grow in the opened canyons and on the bare hillsides a few seasons after the logging-out of The Redwoods; and by the early years of this century people were coming to that part of the county to enjoy the countryside again. This despite continuing depredations by timber cutters, one of whom boasted of cutting seven cords of four-foot firewood from a single unearthed stump.

Meanwhile, between the twilight of the redwoods and the dawn of the railroad, Canyon passed through a fearful and turbulent frontier-gothic night. Isolated and bypassed on the border of a booming county, it became a pocket of homesteaders, squatters, and outcasts, of saloons and land feuds, a full day's ride by horseback from the office of the nearest sheriff. Throughout the 1870's a property dispute raged between the Moraga family, holders of the original grant, on one side, and a series of land grabbers on the other. Shootings, reprisals, pitched battles, cattle thefts, and lawsuits so heated feelings and clouded boundaries that at one time nearly every house on the disputed ground was a fortress of arms and ammunition. Not until 1903 was the question of the Moraga lands finally settled by the U.S. Supreme Court in a decision that involved 19,000 acres. And even then the ownership of Canyon wasn't cleared.

Along Pinehurst Road, on the floor of the canyon near where the Canyon School now stands, was a series of "hotels," actually saloons, with a leaning toward the ancient rustic taste for cruelty to animals: a whisky-drinking pig, a beer-drinking horse, cockfights. According to local legend, the bandit chieftain Joaquin Murietta, a relative of the Moraga family, was a frequent visitor, and at least two men are said to have been lynched at the big oak tree outside Mike Bohan's bar. Curiously enough, the people who look back on these times with a weird, nostalgic relish are among those who are aghast at the looks and habits of the new Young Hairys, who form what they refer to as "the colony."

Settlement ran to a pattern in those days. People would ride out to Canyon in wagons or buggies or on the horse-drawn stage in summer or early fall, when the weather is clear and sunny and less hot than in the surrounding grasslands. Along the creek were the inns where you could eat and drink in cool, dark rustic rooms under the glass eyes of mounted animal heads. There were hollows where you could picnic amid the wood-and-bark shells of ruined redwoods. And, if you were willing to climb the steep hills, you had spectacular views of the surrounding countryside, the Bay, and the Golden Gate. In such circumstances, Canyon seemed a subtropical paradise, an easy, pleasant place to live, where a person might spend half his life outdoors, plow up some land, and plant his own fruit trees and vegetable garden. And when visitors discovered that property was there for the buying, or in some cases for the taking, they often decided that this was where they could live a whole and complete life. So they'd buy land or homestead if they could, but mostly just squat on somebody else's land, build a shack, move in, and make themselves at home.

Until the rain started. Though inland from the Coast Range, Canyon is true Pacific Northwest rain forest, which means that for one or two months of the year, maybe longer, living here is like living under water. It rains when you get up in the morning, and rain is still roaring down when you go to bed at night. It rains heavily yet constantly in a strange, continuous cloudburst that lasts days, then weeks. It rains on your firewood and on your supplies and on your clothesline. The drinking water turns muddy from it, and children get the runs; clothes molder and rot; roofs leak. Everybody has a cold, every child a runny nose. There is mud everywhere, and you have to hand-carry children and supplies up the slippery paths. Occasionally the roads are closed and the creek is swollen. Weakened by the heavy rains, limbs and sometimes whole trees come crashing down on paths and houses. (As recently as 1961, a main road out was blocked for six months by a slide caused by winter rains, and the main automobile bridge across the creek was washed out.)

Day after day the black, oily clouds gather and hang on the lee side of the Oakland hills. It rains here when it doesn't rain anywhere.

When the weather eased to a steady drizzle and the mud began to coagulate, the settlers and squatters would move out, sniffling and sneezing in their damp and dirty clothes, shaking their heads ruefully as their wagons rolled over a hilltop or around a bend into clear, warm sunlight, wondering what in the world they had ever seen in such a gloomy and dreary place. And by spring, Canyon would once again be home to little more than a handful of ranchers, charcoal burners, and saloon keepers.

But what discouraged the settlers was good for the countryside itself. The year-round flow of the creek meant rainbow trout in the winter and fat frogs in summer and spring; and ground squirrels, coyotes, and enormous flocks of wild pigeons thrived in the abundant brush. Hunters and fishermen began coming out to try their luck, and in summer, campers from the increasingly urbanized communities of Oakland and San Francisco. Soon there were whole colonies of tents and shacks where women and children spent their summers, the families of city men who rode out by buggy on weekends. A hotel was built, and there were, of course, the saloons, but when you prepared your cot outdoors in the deep earth silence and looked up at a summer sky in bloom with stars, you could breathe the exquisite luxury of being a long, long way from everywhere.

The railroad came late to Canyon, and it came gently. With the passing of the redwoods, the economy of the East Bay had shifted west, to the manufacturing and shipping towns bordering the Bay itself, and east, to the cattle-and-agriculture country inland. Between the two were the bypassed peaks and valleys, studded now with small trees, of no value commercially except that going there seemed to make people feel good. The railroad saw possibilities in that.

It was called the Oakland, Antioch and Eastern then, a single-track line that emerged from a tunnel in the Oakland hills and followed the creek on the eastern side of the canyon for a few miles before heading inland. Passenger service on the O A & E began in 1913: a steam engine's rhythm echoing in the still can-

yon air, parlor cars with red plush upholstery, uniformed con-
ductors, roadside customers flagging the engineer at stops. All
just twenty minutes from downtown Oakland. The railroad
wanted passengers and started the kind of promotion that
would attract them.

From the utilities district, which already owned considerable
land on the western side of the canyon, the railroad rented picnic areas, which it developed into two large parks, Pinehurst and
Madrone. On weekends special excursion trains ran out to the
parks, and the price of a train ticket included park admission.
Families, business firms, fraternal, religious, and political organizations came out in noisy groups to eat and drink and sometimes
dance on large outdoor floors in the woods. These excursion
trains sometimes ran to fifteen or sixteen cars, and once, a crowd
that numbered in the thousands came out to hear William Jen-
nings Bryan make a campaign speech. The railroad also published a booklet containing maps of the area, with hiking trails
and bridle paths. And on the eastern hillside, the O A & E
began developing real estate.

Along the slopes of the ravine several subdivisions were laid
out: Pinehurst, Canyon City, Moraga Redwood Heights, Hillside Vista Acres. Unlike the familiar mass subdivisions of today,
these developments consisted mostly of summer cottages, built
individually to fit their surroundings—small, comfortable
wooden houses, with large porches to take advantage of views,
trees, and sunlight. The steepness of the hillside made the cutting and filling necessary for elaborate construction prohibitively
expensive, and the scarcity of water placed an absolute limit on
population density. Within ten years, after 110 houses had been
built, development was halted by the lack of water and the inac-
cessibility of the remaining land.

Already, within Canyon, the first notes of a new sort of civic
harmony had been sounded, an idea of community based not on
a religious or social ideology, but on the seemingly contradictory
—and potentially explosive—combination of co-operation and

contentiousness. Out of this clash of opposites came a tone that was the community's own, that would outlast both the railroad and most of the houses, and that would enable Canyon time and again to resist the sad fate of every other rustic town and village in the area.

Probably the school was the start of it. That was when Canyon first began to be more than a summer colony, the kind of place where you would like to live if the world were only otherwise. Beyond the boundaries of other school districts, the community in 1917 organized a school district of its own, levied taxes, chose a school board, hired a teacher, and with donated materials and labor built a one-room Bavarian-cottage-style school, which, since enlarged, stands today in the shadow of 100-foot redwoods. The school represented a personal and financial commitment that had not been made to Canyon before, a willingness to assume responsibility for maintaining and preserving that which is so dispensable to American society at large: the character of the land. It was done when such ideas were not fashionable, it was done in the face of necessity, and it was voluntary. It was an important beginning.

At about the same time, a group of homeowners in the community formed their own water company, the Moraga Heights Mutual Water Commission. The company, still operating today, is owned by the people it serves and is registered with the California Public Utilities Commission. The company has a tunnel up on the hillside with a spring in the back. There is a sump—a main collection point—halfway down the hill, and also a well. Water from all these is pumped to tanks at the top of the hill and distributed from there to fourteen houses. There are water meters, there's a maintenance man who's a resident and part owner, and there is regular billing. No one knows for sure how old the commission is, but the system was in operation as far back as the summer of 1912.

With the coming of these changes, the quality of forethought entered into life in Canyon, but in a limited and unconventional way. People were planning not how large their community might grow, but instead trying to shape its optimum size. Ignoring the common trend of annexation, they were puzzling out ways of keeping Canyon unincorporated and independent. They and their children were to reap a rich reward from their investment.

In those days, you'd see the shoes lined up daily at Pinehurst Station. Hook-type engineer's boots. Rubber waders. Galoshes. Hunter's high-tops. Dusty in summer, mud-caked in winter, standing under waiting-room benches while the feet that walked them this far continued, wing-tipped and pumped, to Oakland, Berkeley, San Francisco. To work, shopping, school. It was twenty minutes to the city, and already there was a cultural gap of thirty years. No sidewalks here, no street lights, no sewers, no gas lines, an inadequate water supply, no firemen, no cops. But a good life, providing you had a taste for it. Those who did— schoolteachers, writers, artists, students, an inventor, business- men, a professional rock collector—identified themselves with the place in which they lived, not by where they worked; and shared a preference for freedom over comfort. Changing shoes might be an inconvenience, but it was preferable to changing Canyon.

For staples there was the Canyon Store. It was run by a coun- try couple, had a potbellied stove in the front room and a slot machine in back. You could buy soap, vegetables, meat, kero- sene, matches—anything you needed. It was a post office and a lending library, and the lady wore a freshly starched apron every day.

The local entertainment was each other. There were picnics in the grove beside the school, potlucks to which every family brought a dish, a white-elephant sort of sale, where children would often buy back the same articles their parents had do- nated, and a big community night on Halloween. And there was visiting. At the end of every nearly vertical stairway and each winding trail was a small, tidy house, where someone would invite you in and offer a cup of tea. The well-worn paths of Canyon are its monument to sociability.

A wood-frame hall had been built behind the store, with a stage and a spring-maple floor from the 1915 Panama-Pacific Exposition in San Francisco. There were plays there occasionally, by and for the members of the community, and all kinds of dances: community dances, square dances, record hops, Gay Nineties, big bands. The hall became the center of most community activities, and the meeting place of the Community Club, the closest thing to a government that Canyon has ever tolerated.

By the beginning of World War Two, Canyon had vegetated into a secluded and largely forgotten retreat, part rustic camp, part resort village, and part commuter town. It was a pleasant place to live, if a bit self-satisfied, with pens of chickens and rabbits, Boy and Girl Scouts, Blue Birds, a Women's Auxiliary, and a Civic Club, the near-realization of every glowing suburban dream.

With the coming of the war, however, Canyon, along with the rest of California, was invaded: but by America, not Japan. The pressure of the flood of thousands of military and war-industry newcomers on the county's available housing forced people to squeeze into Canyon who would have preferred not to live there at all. Wanting to move but unable to build or rent elsewhere, they grumbled at the inconveniences of rustic life, at the winter mud and the steepness of the hills, the abundance of rain and the shortage of drinking water. Like Americans elsewhere in that wartime, they accepted self-denial until, when the war was over, they joined the country's commercial builders in the ranch-house binge that has continued ever since.

Three / Builder

He sits on a bench overlooking a deck made of redwood beams that he has cut and milled himself from trees that had fallen into the creek. The deck forms part of the roof of a huge beam-and-timber skeleton, which he is in the process of turning into a house. The skeleton was condemned in the postings three months before. It adjoins his present house, a weathered wooden structure tucked against the side of a hill, one of the old summer places. That building was condemned six years earlier. There are women and children going in and out of the old house with the random casualness peculiar to the younger element in Canyon. Sleeping bags lie flat and wrinkled on the deck. A blond-haired young man with suspenders and no shirt walks about in a benign daze; he is just back from a year in India. A bearded visitor from Los Angeles sits on the back of the bench, eating a breakfast of bacon, potatoes, and eggs.

There is an open, unbuttoned feeling about the people and the house, as though visitors were expected to drop in at any moment without ceremony or invitation, that seems to stem from a reduction of the necessity to secure property against one's neighbors. Between this plot and the succeeding lands up the hillside, there are no fences; footpaths, winding along the opposite hillside, below the deck, and behind the house, lead across this property to other unfenced houses above. There are no curtains on the windows, no doorbell, no gate. No garage or driveway. No signs forbidding trespass. (At the monthly Canyon Community Club meeting a few nights before, the problem of vandalism had been the subject of long and heated debate. Houses in Canyon had been broken into. Some people wanted warning signs posted; others were for nightly volunteer community patrols. "Great," one Canyon man had commented. "Then we're just like the city, with signs saying DON'T! all over everything and everybody afraid to talk to everybody else." His suggestion about how to avoid vandalism was the only one not rejected by the people present: "Simply don't own anything worth ripping off.")

The owner of the house is a tall, rangy, athletic-looking man with dark brown hair and a mustache, who appears to be in his mid-thirties. He is the president of a successful construction company, but his office is just a desk behind a partition in the large main room of the old house, and when he pulls a rolled architect's drawing down from one shelf, there are battered children's toys and a parlor game on the next, while in the background his wife washes dishes at an ancient, wooden-sideboarded sink. The lines between his life and work are indistinct.

In his faded khakis and faded shirt and scuffed engineer's boots, he has about him the hard vitality of a man who prefers working alongside men to working over them. At a town not far from Canyon, a wealthy man who is much impressed by the revolutionary techniques and materials he uses has contracted with him to build a $100,000 house.

Candid, intelligent, and remarkably broad-minded, he speaks calmly and reflectively of what must have been ugly quarrels and near-desperate circumstances, as if the freedom from drawing lines against trespass within Canyon has been bought at the price of building rigid barriers against trespass from without.

"I bought this house in 1963. I'd heard of Canyon from a friend when I was a student at Pomona. He said that if you ever live around Berkeley, the place to live in is Canyon. The house was condemned when I bought it, so I asked the Building Department for a list of changes necessary to bring it up to code. The list was staggering.

"So, I decided to build a new house instead. But I couldn't get bank financing for the new house because it lacked access. The County Building Department notified me that I had to get out within ten days or they were coming out with bulldozers. My wife was pregnant at the time, and I wasn't going to go. I alerted the newspapers and a TV station, and the day the county was due to come out, I threatened to film the whole thing with a movie camera. The county never came. Eventually, I started work on the new house with my own money. That was how I got to know a lot of the inspectors.

"I had been free-lancing as a carpenter, putting myself through graduate school at Berkeley for an advanced degree in design and sculpture. I started Canyon Construction at the suggestion of a friend of mine who was an investigator for the Contract License Board; he's been a strong influence on me. He suggested that if I wanted to do things myself in my own way, the only sensible method was to go into business on my own and do it legally. He convinced me of the value of being licensed, of how it would give me better collective power. I dislike business detail, haggling and wheedling, and I decided that this method was the easiest way of minimizing it. I work out of my home as a licensed building contractor and do work both in Canyon and out of it. My employees are about ten to one Canyon residents. For some reason, Canyon is loaded with carpenters. That and Indian musicians. We get all the work we want and try to limit the work to six months a year. I pay top wages, but my men don't belong to any unions, more out of a dislike of outside interference than anything else.

"I've done about six construction jobs in Canyon. Canyon Construction built the post office and supervised the remodeling of the store. Because I know the building inspectors personally, I've been able to talk to them in behalf of people here, and I've helped get clearance for jobs when supposedly none was available. In the middle of the postings, for example, the electrical wiring in one of the homes gave out, and I found it was a mess. By saying the house was a fire hazard, I got an inspector to come out and indicate what corrections were necessary to bring the house up to code. Then I made the corrections.

"I have great hopes for some of the newer, younger men in the county departments in terms of their attitudes toward Canyon and the quality of life generally. Knowing them as individuals, I feel there's hope for bringing them around. Inspectors, for instance, can and do—with exceptions—recognize honest intentions. Again, with exceptions, they realize that there is no other community so solidly behind improving itself at its own expense, people using their own work and their own land. They can see that we have a high degree of participation here, and they know that's a rare thing. The problem is that the Health Department, the Building Department, and the Zoning Department are all headed by men who floated to the top out of seniority and have been in their jobs since the forties. Behind them are better-trained, more able, more active personalities, who are really the guts of their departments. I work on my relationships with these younger men.

"As for the postings, they were actually triggered by a formal complaint filed by some of the older residents about illegal building. The Supervisor representing our district pressed the Building Department to crack down. And they did.

"I can sympathize with the way some of the older people feel. They've lost the community as they built and fought for it. One man built the road practically by hand with a wheelbarrow. He and another man built their homes themselves, everything from pouring concrete to nailing shingles. Now the community has changed. New people are running *their* Community Club. New kids are in the school, not *their* kids. The older people don't feel safe because of changes in the community. They see people sleeping in the grass, and they assume people are shitting in the grass, and they are probably right. People are around in various stages of undress. Some nude. Their hang-up is a genuine one, and I feel bad about it. But I see no way to change it. I try to give the older people due respect, but you can't turn things back, particularly where individual human behavior is concerned."

Four / The Solution
to Pollution

A mile and a half from Canyon, across a warped and rattling highway bridge, is a grassy hollow leading to the edge of Upper San Leandro Reservoir. In the hollow is the trace of a road and an odd variety of mature trees, but mostly just fenced-off grassland with white-faced cattle eating, numb and distant. This is Valle Vista, once a community of a dozen houses with landscaping and small orchards and a railroad station, now fenced and posted watershed property of the East Bay Municipal Utilities District. At one time, Valle Vista and Canyon enjoyed the same surroundings, the same school, and the same way of life. They very nearly suffered the same death.

In July of 1951, on the recommendation of the State Department of Public Health, the Board of Directors of East Bay MUD announced that they had adopted a policy of buying land in Canyon as it came up for sale, because seepage from Canyon septic tanks was polluting San Leandro Creek and threatening the county water supply.

Though not admitted publicly at the time, the ultimate aim of the utilities district was to obtain complete title to the Canyon area and turn it into fenced-off watershed or controlled park and recreation land. In effect, to sanitize it. Conceived by engineers, instigated by the utilities district's Sanitation Department, the policy was pursued with mathematical absoluteness, and East Bay MUD began making an automatic offer on any piece of property that was, or even might be, available in Canyon, just because it was there.

According to John Plumb, Secretary of East Bay MUD, "Any watershed that has septic tanks on it which are that old is a hazard. This is a working procedure in any water agency in the United States. Any waterman with a creek with septic tanks above it would be a fool if he didn't worry about it."

East Bay MUD's engineers did worry about it; maybe too much, Plumb now concedes. "Our engineers were perhaps taking an uptight position, on which they could have bent."

Surprisingly, the utilities district initiated its land-purchase program without first taking a bacteriological test of the contamination levels of the water in the creek.

"We just didn't sample and plot things in 1950–55," says Gordon Laverty, then an East Bay MUD sanitation engineer and now manager of the utilities district's water services. "Only when the residents became more sophisticated did we become more sophisticated."

Instead, when confronted with occasional skeptical grumbling on the part of individuals in Canyon, East Bay MUD engineers responded by arranging public demonstrations, which were at best inconclusive and, at worst, low-comic parodies of scientific method.

To demonstrate the contamination caused by seepage from Canyon septic tanks, East Bay MUD officials in the late 1940's placed chemical dyes in two toilets less than sixty feet from the creek. The toilets were outside the Canyon Dance Hall, which at the time had a crowd of nearly 600 customers, and a high percentage of beer drinkers. The utilities district engineers waited for traces of the chemicals to appear in the creek. And waited. Until after months of sampling and observation, the test was discontinued.

Next, dyes were put in every septic tank in the community, on the assumption that saturation of ground cover had produced pollution. But Canyon stands on vertical-strata shale, a sort of natural filter that, combined with septic tanks, can be extremely effective at treating bacteria. Again, no trace of the dyes ever appeared in the creek.

One Health Department officer, scooping up a test tube full of water from the creek, dropped a chemical into it and told the Canyon postmistress, standing by, to "watch this turn blue." It didn't.

Not until the summer of 1967, when the composition of the community had completely changed and the local posture had stiffened with individual unwillingness to be infringed upon, was the utilities district challenged to prove that the creek was, in fact, contaminated.

"We were willing to go that route," says Laverty. "Throughout the month of August, we sampled the creek above Canyon, at the post office (the midpoint of the community), and below. And our data indicates that the creek is contaminated. The count averaged 2,500 coliform-bacteria organisms per milliliter, varying from a low of 2,000 to as high as 6,000. The maximum to swim in is 1,000 organisms per milliliter.

"After a weekend, the bacterial count in the creek rose dramatically, and at first we didn't know what to make of it. Then we realized that Canyon has an influx of people on weekends—visitors, children home from school—and that they were flushing more contamination into the ground. It comes right through the thin mantle of soil and into the creek. And it's consistent with people's habits."

Another sample, taken by an independent chemist retained by residents of Canyon, and representing a laboratory certified by the State Department of Public Health, produced a conflicting conclusion.

The Solution to Pollution

According to the chemist, Harry D. Kiplinger, the creek waters are fairly heavily contaminated from cattle-raising operations in the unpopulated areas above Canyon, and the coliform-bacteria count actually decreases as the creek runs past the community itself.

"The pattern of the results," concludes Kiplinger, "shows no particular increase in bacterial counts due to human occupancy up and down the two-and-a-half-mile run of the creek. To maintain that contamination is caused by any use of the ravine by humans, particularly where any wastes are conveyed and treated in a way satisfactory to the County Health Department, is totally groundless."

The two tests were made on samples from the same stretch of the creek, taken during the same month: August, 1967.

"Taking samples doesn't prove anything," says Ted M. Gerow, Contra Costa County's Chief of Environmental Health. "Bacterial counts can vary from one week to the next, and we can't differentiate between animal and human waste. The real proof is what you see and what you mechanically determine."

"I walked the hills," says Laverty, "and I saw raw sewage coming out of the hillside. You could see [in the early 1950's] septic tanks discharging directly into the creek."

That was sufficient proof for the utilities district. In 1952 alone, East Bay MUD bought twenty-four houses in Canyon, burned them down, and bulldozed their foundations. The utilities district became the largest property owner in the community.

The property was acquired lot by lot. A man representing East Bay MUD would come around in Canyon occasionally, using scare tactics: sell or get condemned. But the land wasn't all acquired by threats. Sometimes people who wanted to sell approached the district. Unlike other prospective buyers, the utilities district paid cash. And people, especially older people, often called East Bay MUD first when they wanted to sell, preferring cash in hand to monthly payments.

The buying-up of Canyon property continued even after the houses that had been observed discharging directly into the creek had been eliminated. According to East Bay MUD's John Plumb, the dangers of water pollution didn't diminish arithmetically.

"Half the original homes are not half the threat that a hundred and ten homes were. On a watershed, we would be concerned if there was one house, if it was unsewered and within a thousand feet of a tributary to a reservoir."

This 1,000-foot radius includes just about every house in Canyon.

It wasn't that the people of Canyon were unwilling to connect with a conventional sewer system; it was just that the physical and financial burden of doing so would have broken the community. To tie into a normal gravity sewer would have meant paying for the installation of a full five miles of main from the nearest town, plus connections to each house. On top of this, the loss of ground water through an outside sewer system would require the community to pipe in water the same distance. The cost of bringing in water alone was estimated at twenty-eight dollars per foot for the full five miles, prohibitive for such a small number of homes.

Throughout the 1950's and into the 1960's, houses all up and down the hillside continued to be razed. The community shrank to less than half its former size, and the work force declined drastically. Worst of all, there was a tendency among the remaining residents to accept what was happening as inevitable.

As Canyon declined, Valle Vista disappeared. There the utilities district, having acquired all the houses, demolished them and fenced off the land, leaving Valle Vista just pasture and a name on the map. East Bay MUD officials, accused by people in Canyon of land grabbing, mendacity, and political persecution, insist that the company's only interest has always been the prevention of pollution, and that if the Canyon houses could somehow be brought up to Health Department codes, they would be satisfied. But when people from Canyon, passing by the vacant, grassy hollow on the highway to Moraga, look at what remains of Valle Vista, they see the future East Bay MUD has in mind for them.

For a time, the older residents didn't realize that there were new people coming into Canyon, people with the light-traveling look of transients but with a firm desire to stay. There had always been a flow of visitors up and down the Redwood Highway, Canyon's lone paved road; and occasionally young people had camped in the grove beside the school or up on the hillside for a day or two and then moved on. During the fifties there had been a few beatnik types with long hair and motorcycles, but they had been more interested in remaining in motion than in putting down roots. In the sixties, though, when certain sets of hair and motorcycles began to seem familiar and children began to appear, and old cars and litter and junk, and dogs running around wild, and finally when these newcomers began to attract publicity, even the most sheltered old-timer knew that Canyon was changing.

In the long winter of its decline, the community had become cut off, so isolated from the urban centers nearby that people who stumbled on Canyon were often astonished that a place so undeveloped could exist just over the hills from Oakland.

In truth, Canyon was just about as remote as it appeared. The railroad, renamed the Sacramento-Northern, discontinued passenger service in 1940 and went out of business in the late 1950's, disappearing, tracks and all, and leaving Canyon without any public transportation whatsoever, as it remains to this day. The parks and picnic grounds, which had increased to three, were now fenced off by East Bay MUD, and the buildings and dance floors were razed. The store, which changed hands several times during this period, eventually lost its permit to sell produce, whereupon both store and dance hall deteriorated into a sagging, frayed, vandalized shambles. Canyon was no longer

35

such a nice place to visit. But there were still people who wanted to live there.

Where did they come from, these inland castaways, with their unkempt hair and clothing, thumbing along the suburban roads and handling the oranges in the Moraga Safeway? Standing barefoot in the shopping-center hardware store, or sitting, pregnant and ringless, in the Moraga Laundromat. Looking ferocious and acting benign. What was it they were after out here?

They came from among the elite of the world's most technically civilized culture, and they were seeking within it the possibility of living a less corrupt, more simple, more innocent life.

Turning away from the plagues of civilization, competition, egotism, exploitation, inequality, joyless labor, they came by routes of varying seriousness or self-realization upon the unyielding fact of property. And concluded that to attempt to separate oneself from the existing social structure required binding oneself to a particular piece of land. Starting two, three, many Waldens.

This they had in common, and a few other things. A feeling for nature that was to some degree romantic; a willingness to work hard toward their own ends, combined with a general indifference to physical inconvenience; in many cases, highly developed and marketable skills; and in all but a few, an encounter at some point with the life and ideas of Berkeley.

In the early nineteen sixties, Berkeley became Canyon's window on the outside world. Half of Berkeley, it was said, wanted to live in Canyon, and a small but steady stream of hitchhikers flowed back and forth between the two communities on either side of the Oakland hills. In Canyon, "going to town" came to mean going to one town only.

Always an individualistic community, even among university towns, Berkeley was the epicenter for many of the seismic changes that were to rock American life throughout the latter half of the sixties. The free-speech movement, university demonstrations, the peace movement, some important new music, the hippies, and later the Yippies all spread in some degree from Berkeley. But these shock waves of expression, as they became increasingly massive and organized, seemed to some Berkeley individualists to acquire many of the faults of the lumbering, arbitrary social structure they had sought to shake off. So, acting by preference as individuals, they began turning away from mass movements aimed at improving society at large to the more personal and perhaps more radical pursuit of meaningful work, life, and community. While they had opted out of mass-action politics, it was not for the popular alternative of psychedelic solipsism. In moving to Canyon, they had not only moved out of The Movement but had dropped out of Dropping Out.

They were graduate students and university staff, lab technicians and teaching assistants, street people and dissatisfied undergraduates, kids who had grown up in Berkeley and gone away to school but had now returned. Unlike most Americans, who accept that the confines of job and career will largely determine where and how they live, they sought first to establish the quality of individual life. And unlike the cult-and-commune faddists of the late sixties, most of them remained independent of each other by continuing in school or maintaining jobs outside the community.

Those who could afford to bought land and old houses, usually with the last cent of their savings, and these homes became homes to their friends, too, places where they could spend a night away from Berkeley or wayside lodgings between sister communities like Big Sur and Mendocino. If one of these friends decided to stay in Canyon and wanted to build a shelter or a one-room shack, he could usually find someone who would let him have a corner of land, as well as people who would show him how to build, help him find materials, and lend him tools. This helped produce some remarkably inventive and individualistic architecture: geodesic domes, tree houses, and lightweight, cheap, or castoff materials used in original ways.

In this manner, the new community began to grow rather like

a family, acquaintances becoming in-laws after a subtle process of testing and approval. As in most families, there was a set of implicit assumptions. It helped you get into Canyon if you had school-age children or if your moving in somehow meant increased business for the post office. There were enemies—the county and East Bay MUD. And rules: doing your own thing was okay; shooting guns and building fires were not. All this made up a body of unofficial law and a set of values unique to the community. Going naked, for example, is less objectionable in Canyon than shooting guns.

The population was climbing again. There were pregnant women on the paths and children in the school and willing hands when there was work to be done. When the Road Association, a closed group of older residents that finances and maintains the Redwood Highway, posted a call for volunteers for its annual Work Day, there was a turnout of young people, not Association members, that was almost embarrassing. And, at the monthly Community Club meetings in the Canyon School, the percentage of newcomers had grown so large that they threatened to take over the club entirely.

The Club President, sensing what was coming, tried to persuade the older people to come to the meetings and meet the newcomers face to face. They came maybe three or four times, and some of the differences between the new Canyon and the old Canyon were brought out into the open. The problems of noise and litter and junked cars and garbage and unleashed dogs. There was wrangling and name-calling, but people were able to get a lot of things off their chests. If it had continued, the discussion might have confined the division between the residents to the community. Instead, the older people withdrew, leadership of the Community Club fell to the young, the line between the two was clearly defined, and their differences intensified.

Five / Backwoodsman

About eleven o'clock on a Saturday morning, the old cars and jeeps begin pulling up outside the red-white-and-blue trailer that serves as the Canyon Post Office, and Canyon's young people, three, four, six piling out of each vehicle, stream up and down the trailer's steps, opening mail, exchanging news, gossip, invitations, in a scene reminiscent of the institutional spontaneity of a campus student union.

Minutes later, six of these people, all from the upper part of Canyon where the new houses are being built, drive on down Pinehurst Road almost to the beginning of utilities-district land and, turning up a little-used dirt road, stop outside one of the old summer houses, run-down, behind a neglected, weed-grown garden with cross-pollinating fruit trees.

They crowd into the house, talking, joking, making plans for co-operative errands, shopping for bargains at Sears or Simon Brothers Wreckers or Ward's, going to the Laundromat, buying and hauling building materials. You notice that no one in the community seems to ever wear a watch.

"This is Rachael," says the man who owns the house, intro-

Canyon

ducing a girl who is about seven months' pregnant. "Rachael is Mike's chick. Mike's in Santa Rita." Rachael is blooming with the beauty of pregnancy and is aware that she is being looked after; it is an essential reassurance in a community where no comfort can be taken for granted. The previous summer, one young Canyon woman, exasperated when, while she was pregnant, the spring supplying her house ran dry, moved to San Francisco to have her baby and returned to Canyon only after considerable persuasion.

"It's not so bad really," says Rachael. "When water is short, you go to somebody else's house to take a shower, and you post a sign that says 'Don't flush for number one' over the toilet."

She explains how cooking among the younger people is done on wood-and-coal or butane stoves because it is impossible to get electric service without a building permit, and the rates are more than double what they are in the city.

"To do dishes," says another girl, with the wholesome, steely prettiness of a campus queen, "you heat a small amount of water, then mix the heated water with cold and rinse with cold. People all lived this way not so very long ago, and they got by fine.

"Most people go to Laundromats in Moraga or Orinda to wash their clothes," she continues. "Canyon has no sidewalks and often a good deal of mud or dust, and our hands or feet are often dirty. So suburban people look down their noses at the 'dirty hippies.' "

They talk about their difficulties with the county and with officials' involvement in real-estate deals, and about a Supervisor's rumored personal vendetta against Canyon. They ask if you're interested in buying a house, in moving into the community. ("How old's your kid? Six? There are five girls here that age. He'd get laid like crazy.") After a while, they begin to drift away on their arranged errands until only the man who owns the house and the pregnant girl remain.

He is a restless, mordant, caustic man, with bushy, curly hair and a bulldozed-earth mustache, who speaks and moves as if he had been plucked off a Brooklyn street corner that morning and flown west. Born in Brownsville, a former physics student and instructor at Brandeis and Berkeley, he now teaches a humanities course at a San Francisco art school.

He and his wife and young daughter have had one house burned out from over them in Canyon and outbid East Bay MUD for the one they live in now, although he had to go to court to do it. Proudly, he displays the news clipping: "HIPPIE OUTBIDS EBMUD FOR PARCEL."

Inside, the house is mostly vacant, furnished in Old Miscellaneous: rump-sprung sofa, hand-me-down table, bare floors. For a man who lives on the edge of a wilderness, he seems remarkably deficient in handicrafts. Perhaps that is why he values them so little.

"Like, nobody can *do* anything. That's the doctrine, right? There's this big mystique surrounding the performance of skills, and it's a deliberate shuck. I was in physics, and I know. There are easier ways to do things than they want to let you know. All those linear equations. I mean, in the city you believe that water comes from the water company, not from the mountains. Or that bread comes from Langendorf, so nobody should strike. Or that we should stay in Vietnam because the Pentagon says there's no way out."

Pacing, fidgeting, he ransacks the pockets of his pants, his shirt, then pulls a drawer out of the table. Excusing himself, he walks outside into the yard and begins stalking back and forth, looking at the ground. He picks up something, looks at it, throws it down, repeating this perhaps a dozen times before finding what he wants. Then he comes inside, holding the small, snipped butt of a roach, which he lights, and resumes pacing.

"The evidence accumulated by all competent biologists and ecologists says we're moving toward an enormous disaster to our civilization. I mean, the figures are there. Like, people are going to be tapping pipes for buckets of water—ripping it off. The possibility of surviving as individuals and communities is bound up with the possibility of rebuilding civilization along ecological lines.

"It's already started to happen here. East Bay MUD says that if they buy the land here, they're going to turn it over to the Regional Park District. That's what they said in Wildcat Canyon, and they sold that to developers. They want this for real estate, and the Supervisors are in on it. Three out of the five Directors of East Bay MUD live in the constituency of the President of the Board of Supervisors.

"When I outbid the water company for this place, they didn't expect that there would be anyone bidding against them, so they sent their man to probate court with a fixed amount. But the law says that estates sold by executors automatically go to the highest bidder. Were they shook when we topped their bid! Then we said we were ready to go even higher. That shook them even more. The judge said that buyers were required to put down a cash deposit in estate bidding. That was when I turned over a cashier's check for the full amount. The place was in turmoil. But we got the property, over two acres and three houses."

A man in Canyon who knew him well in Berkeley says that he has moved to Canyon because it is a smaller pond and he a bigger fish. Listening to him, laughing with him, you can't help wondering if he has found his home in Canyon, or in protest.

"Actually, Canyon is just a way station for me on the road to something more tolerable. I'm trying to organize a commune in British Columbia as an ecological redoubt. Some property one mile square has been picked out. There aren't any roads, but there's everything you need. A group of people are going to work on it during vacations preparatory to moving there permanently. The commune would be an entirely self-contained economic unit. We'd raise our own food, generate our own power, build with our own hands using natural materials.

"I'd be going right now except for one thing. I have to go into the hospital and have this hernia operation."

Six / Resistance

☆ Early on Thanksgiving morning, 1967, the Canyon Store and Dance Hall have the slack, gray look of the truly condemned awaiting a final indignity: bulldozer, arsonist's match, or falling tree. Every window in the store is broken. The roof is gap-shingled and sagging. A wall of siding is gone, exposing pale interior paper, frayed wiring, legs of furniture, corroded pipe, and piled debris in a vivid, one-building flash of slum. In this instance, the county condemnation notice seems an understatement.

The sky is overcast. The trees are dripping, and there is ice on the stack of new lumber beside the store. After they walk down from the hillside, the first of the men put aside their picks and saws and sledges and build a fire in a steel drum and gather around it, rubbing their hands and trying to keep warm. Other men join them. They wear beards, mustaches, coveralls, odd hats—Stetsons, coonskins, Navy watch caps. A woman brings a pot of coffee and cups, and the men stand for a while drinking coffee and talking close to the fire. Then, led by the man from Canyon Construction, the crew goes to work: they remove salvageable fixtures, window frames, shingles, doors; rip at the walls with crowbars, picks, sledges, and chain saws; strip away laths, knock the supports loose, and, in a group, heave the walls flat. More of the community begins to arrive, women in jeans and men's shirts, children in parkas and ponchos. A demolition line is organized to pass dismantled lumber from person to person and onto a pile. Nobody works too hard. There is a lot to be done, but there will be plenty of people to do it, and the job itself is a social event. The rural resistance has begun. Denied a permit to rebuild the Canyon Store, the community has mobilized to do it anyway, illegally. ☆

Months before, without open discussion and under a veiled wording of its agenda, the Board of Directors of East Bay MUD had voted to acquire and tear down the Canyon Store, post office, and dance hall, cutting off access to Pinehurst Road and eliminating the heart of the community's social life. The store's owner, a former Canyon resident who had been unable to operate or lease her property, had accepted East Bay MUD's negotiated price only as a last resort.

When word of the proposed purchase filtered back to Canyon, the residents were shocked and angry. Though the dance hall was no longer operating, the post office and store were still the one place where everyone went daily, where news and gossip were exchanged and notes were posted. To tear them down would leave Canyon little more than a school and some isolated houses in the woods.

That evening three of the older residents who had remained active in the community called an emergency meeting at the Canyon School. They agreed to form a Store Trust, pledging their own savings plus whatever they could borrow or beg, to raise the amount necessary to meet the utilities district's bid. One man, bringing up seven children on a civil-service salary, pledged $1,000. Another man, no wealthier, put up $1,000 and agreed to do the legwork. A woman who had lived in Canyon for twenty years put up $2,000 and promised to keep the books.

From this beginning, the Canyon Store Trust, in the space of a few weeks, raised $14,000, or approximately $100 for every man, woman, and child in the community. They then made a counteroffer for the store, which the woman who owned it promptly accepted.

For the first time, the community had bid against the utilities district for a parcel of property, effectively acting in behalf of its own survival, and had won. What had seemed inevitable, the fate of Valle Vista and Pinehurst and Madrone and a thousand other rustic communities in metropolitan America, was not quite inevitable after all. The store and dance hall were now officially the property of the Canyon Store Trust and of the community. The County Health Department immediately condemned it.

☆ By Thanksgiving afternoon the store is reduced to a skeleton, and the dance hall is gone. A bonfire has been started, and the scrapped material is burning. The sun has come out, and some of the workmen have stripped off their shirts. There is a washtub of cold beer and a big, steaming pot of stew, which a girl is ladling onto paper plates. Children are dangling from the trees; dogs pursue one another and snarl over a stick. Apart from the demolition, men are building wooden forms and mixing and pouring concrete, hauling water up in buckets from the creek and pouring it into the mixer, while the man from Canyon Construction puts down his sledge and refers to his plans. ☆

The original blueprints submitted to the county had been for a complete Canyon Community Center, including an assembly hall, a new store containing a residence, and a new post-office building. Approved by the County Planning Commission, the permit was denied by the Board of Supervisors in response to a request by East Bay MUD. First of all, they insisted, a full and complete study was necessary concerning Canyon's water supply, fire and police protection, garbage disposal, traffic regulation, and zoning. Also, what about this question of flower chil-

46

dren? Runaways from other communities had begun turning up in Canyon. Wouldn't this new community center become a haven for them? There were to be public toilets there.

Behind the immediate issue of the community center was the larger question of the straight world's relationship to "hippie types," of fundamentally opposing views as to the quality and character of future life in Canyon. It loaded every question with emotional feelings and ideological overtones, and made every decision a deliberate weighing of political and social consequences.

Useless to the community, the old store grew increasingly dilapidated from month to month, more and more of an eyesore, and an invitation to anyone with a touch of vandalism passing by on the road. It was only a matter of time until someone got hurt around there or the whole structure collapsed.

In answer to East Bay MUD's objections, Canyon Construction and the Store Trust agreed to submit a revised plan and to work with the Health Department in determining a proper sanitation system. After studying the situation, the Health Department's Chief Engineer admitted that the only feasible system was underground storage: a septic tank. To East Bay MUD, this was totally unacceptable.

But there was still a possibility that the system might be approved over the utilities district's objections if the Health Department was satisfied. Canyon might yet get its community center.

☆ At night the store is floodlit, and a small crew of men continues to work under the lights. People stand around the bonfire watching, drinking coffee and wine, smoking and talking. A full fifty-man crew has turned out to work on Thanksgiving Day, and most will be back tomorrow. The upper floor of the store will be jacked up and a new foundation and a new lower floor put in. If all goes well, come Monday morning the county authorities will have quite a surprise. ☆

Canyon

The modified plan had called for only minor changes—remodeling the store, tearing down the dance hall behind it, and building a new post office. When this plan was rejected, it seemed obvious to the people in Canyon that the county authorities were not going to approve any remodeling of the Canyon Store. East Bay MUD officials had conceded that the matter was to be a showdown concerning the whole question of septic tanks in watershed lands. In effect, a showdown for Canyon as a community. Without remodeling, the store was worthless and would undoubtedly be subject to abatement proceedings as a nuisance. To simply accept this was to accept the loss of all local control over the community's survival and conclude, as did one county official who, referring to Canyon, said that "some communities just have to go."

In the face of so drastic a situation, the work party had been a snap to organize. First there was Canyon Construction. All the men who regularly worked for it helped with the remodeling of the store, providing the necessary experience and supervision and requisitioning most of the building material. Then there were the men who had moved into Canyon and picked up some construction skills in the process of building or renovating their own homes. There were the community's remarkably accomplished women, who brought coffee, wine, and beer; fixed casseroles, beans, salad, bread, cold cuts, and cheese; drove jeeps and trucks up and down the hill, worked in the demolition line, and helped put up tar paper and insulation. There were the children, some of whom had built their own tree houses and were more than capable of doing a grown man's work. And there were the friends, contractors who came from San Francisco and as far away as Sacramento, bringing lumber, siding, and panes of glass. There were even a few total strangers, passing by on the road, who parked their cars and pitched in, only to leave at the end of the work day, knowing they'd probably never see any of these people again.

48

☆ By Sunday afternoon the store is once again upright and angular. The sag is out of the roof, the shagginess is gone, the windows and siding and shingles have been replaced, the joints fit. Finished work—the installation of fittings and paneling and checking the level of beams—is being done by a few of the more experienced construction men, while a crowd of people has gathered by the bonfire, staring in a sort of self-congratulatory daze at what they have accomplished. Not a new store, but a genuine restoration, an external realization of their community and themselves. Like them, it belongs. Someone has hand-lettered an appropriately rustic sign: CANYON GENERAL STORE AND TRADING POST, SINCE 1897. It is hung prominently on the side of the building. *Now* let the county come. ☆

It wasn't the building itself that was so offensive to the county authorities. That was rather pleasant, actually, a two-story frame building with stained-wood siding and shingles and latticework windows, patterned on the classic country store—not that far-out architecture like the pads up on the hill. It preserved local tradition and represented the elimination of a public hazard. Privately, some individuals in the Health Department were willing to admit that the Canyon people and their helpers had done one hell of a job. But the *way* it was done, the childish defiance of legal authority, the hicklike barn-raising way the work was organized, a bunch of hippies playing pioneer. Was that really necessary? After all, there were perfectly legal methods of getting work like this done, appeals you could make, county boards who could have worked out a compromise satisfactory to all parties, bonds you could sell to raise money. But they seemed to feel they had to do it this way, to demonstrate that they could rebuild their store themselves and make it work. Now the job was done, and it seemed to have taken on a permanent character. People were already receiving their mail at the store, and there were plans for installing counters and cold-storage bins.

49

East Bay MUD was hopping mad. Their concerns about Canyon, after all, were genuine. They simply couldn't have human pathogens in a reservoir. So something had to be done, and done now.

A STOP WORK notice was posted on the building immediately, threatening arrests if more work was done. And there was still the county health code that must be met; in its present state, the store couldn't qualify for a license. A new sewer system would have to be installed first, and they'd need permits for that. Then, even if the work was finished and approved, they'd have to apply for permits to operate the store, to sell food and alcoholic beverages. Thumbing your nose at the county could prove to be a very expensive gesture.

A new sewer system. A new septic tank, pipes, a pump system: that would take money. A forty-foot absorption pit: a bulldozer would be needed. The community already owed money for the reconstruction of the store. Now it must spend more or let the delay and decay begin all over again. They'd raise the money somehow. What about the work, though? The notice on the building threatened arrests. But they wouldn't be working on the building itself, only on the ground beside it. And they would pick a time when everybody in Canyon was available and the police were busy elsewhere. New Year's.

☆ On New Year's weekend, 1968, the work crew is mobilized again. Picks and shovels this time. Rakes and hoes. A bulldozer is there, and a Ford trencher, a Canyon kid riding up beside the operator, who is a friend of Canyon Construction. In three days, the digging is done, a new tank is lowered into the pit, pipes and a pump system are installed. While a surveyor puts in the grades, a landscape architect directs the location and planting of small trees. At night, once again there is a bonfire. And on the afternoon of the third day, when the system is finished and the bulldozer operator stands ready to push the fill into the trenches and the pit, work is halted. Film and still photographs have been taken of every stage of construction, particularly of the pit, to show the shale base of Canyon's soil. Now, before the system is covered, calls go out to the utilities district, the Health Department, and the Building Department, inviting them to send inspectors out to make whatever suggestions or corrections they feel are necessary. Only the utilities-district men come. As they watch, the bulldozer is started, the pits and trenches filled, and the job completed. ☆

According to Canyon Construction, the men from East Bay MUD couldn't find anything in the work itself to disagree with. According to Gordon Laverty, the scene represented something with which he couldn't have disagreed more.

"They had directly flouted the law to dig a ditch for the community-center septic tank. All the excavation proved was that raw sewage was going to go directly into the creek through fractured layers of shale. They had replaced a tank that was already discharging directly into the creek. But there it was, an accomplished fact."

Faced with the reality of a new Canyon Post Office and a new Canyon Store, the authorities of Contra Costa County reluctantly granted the permits to build them.

Seven / Citizen

By all the rules of politics and stereotypes, he should be the avowed enemy of Canyon's encroaching young: clean-shaven, in his fifties, a Canyon resident for more than twenty years, father of seven daughters, President of the District School Board and of the Moraga Heights Mutual Water Commission, last of the old residents to serve as President of the Community Club, he, more than any other single person, embodies what was settled and stable about the old Canyon. Yet he is closest to the new. Almost alone among the older members of the community, he has changed and grown, though his support of changes has cost him friends.

His house is one of the old summer places, a half-rebuilt mixture of natural wood and tar paper. The interior is cluttered but comfortable, and organized around a wood-and-coal stove and furnace in the main room, a combination living room, dining room, and kitchen. He sits in a rocker amid a pleasant scattering of magazines, toys, and school work, puffing paternally on his pipe, two of his younger daughters clinging shyly near him as he talks with wry pride about his oldest daughter, who has just won a college scholarship. ("Only way she could afford to go.")

The center of his pride in the community is the Canyon

School. Small, intimate, peculiarly responsive to Canyon, the school reserves the first two hours of each day for quiet study, the teachers occasionally hold discussions on walks among the trees, individual advancement is encouraged, and there is a file in which parents may check their children's progress at any time. In 1968, out of a student body of thirty-one, the school had five children identified as gifted under California's state program.

"We have a pretty good thing here," the School Board President says. "And we know it."

After a while, a couple from farther up the road, who look to be in their forties, stop by, dropping in to visit and watch television—the way people visited each other in the early fifties. The TV is turned on, and gradually the girls and the visitors are drawn to it, while the man who owns the house rocks, pulls meditatively on his pipe, and talks.

The younger people say that he has worked on more community projects than anybody else, and one man who spent several Saturdays working along with him, putting finishing touches on the rebuilt store, treasures the moments they spent working together as among the best of his life. Another man, bearded, beaded, sandaled, puts it this way: "I never had a father. But if I *had* a father, that's the man I'd want my father to be."

Asked to explain his extraordinary rapport with the community's young people, he says that it is due to an open-mindedness toward people generally that he has developed in the course of his job. He has been employed, for more than twenty years, as a criminal investigator for the Oakland Naval Supply Depot.

"In 1946, just after I got out of the service, I was living in Alameda with my aunt. I had a dog, and after a while the dog began to get on my aunt's nerves. I put an ad in the Alameda paper advertising for a place to live. A man responded who didn't even take the paper—somebody had thrown it on his porch. He had a place in Canyon that he hadn't seen in years. He wasn't even sure he could find it. I came out, saw the house, and rented it for ten dollars a month. Eventually I offered to buy it. He wanted twenty-five hundred dollars, which was more than I could pay. I found a place just across the road for seventeen hundred and bought it. That was this place.

"I had grown up in the county and knew the area a little from when I was a boy. We used to picnic, my folks tell me, at Pinehurst Park. That's down by the Y in the road leading to Moraga. It's water-company land now, but you can see the remains of picnic tables and the foundations of a bandstand.

"There were close to three hundred people in Canyon then—more than there are now. Most people had come here through friends, during or after the war, when housing was short.

"About 1948 or 1949, a water-company representative came down to the Community Club meeting and suggested that the residents should request to have the community rezoned to half-acre residential land to control building and that this would resolve the water company's worries about pollution. This the people did. They petitioned the county and had Canyon rezoned half-acre residential. Less than a year later the water company started hollering about contamination and buying up property. They never would have been stopped if it hadn't been for some of the younger people.

"I guess the big difference between my relationship with the younger element in the community and that of the other older residents stems from the fact that I permitted myself to become acquainted with the young people. And rather got to like their attitudes.

"In the old days the Canyon Store was a regular general store. It sold beer and wine and groceries. The proprietor eventually became my father-in-law. I had a bunch of dogs in those days and bought maybe a hundred pounds of dog food a week there. The dance hall was leased out two or three times a week. Even then the water company was trying to prove contamination, and they never could—with many more people coming out than come now.

54

"The night we decided to buy the store I came home and told my wife that I had promised to put a thousand dollars into the Canyon Store Trust. She said we didn't have a thousand dollars. I said then we'd have to borrow it, which we did.

"I'm actually the maintenance man for the Water Commission. I go around reading meters. We've run out of water for short periods of time, usually in September or October. A pipe will break, or someone will go away on vacation and leave a faucet running. When the water runs out, you just have to wait until it comes back. Canyon has more water now than before—there are fewer people, and we have improved the system. When I first got here, rationing got down to sixty gallons a day —and it takes five gallons just to flush a toilet. In recent times it hasn't been as low as that.

"We don't want to lose the post office or the school. We don't want to lose our homes. But now there are all these problems with the authorities. Everything is an emotional issue now. Some people are against things just because of the people who are for them. It's like the trouble with the road. Some people were upset about the increased traffic. There was talk of putting up a gate, but there were legal problems involved. The gate had to be down one full day a year. So one of the younger people put up a bar at the bottom of the road. All you had to do was bump it and it moved. People were against it, just because of the man who put it up.

"I know that almost anything I need I could ask someone here for and get it. A couple of the younger people worked all day on my house once when a tree had fallen on it. As for the store, I knew the kids would raise the money if I asked them.

"It's hard for people to understand that in our democracy you can be against something that other people are for and not hate them personally. Person to person the water-company officials are easy to deal with. The trouble is with corporate practices over which they have no control."

Eight/Doing It the Way You're Not Supposed To

In the grove beside the school, about where the baseball backstop used to be, a massive web-work dome, made of old railroad ties held together by welded steel plates, all based on tension and compression, everything leaning against everything else, looking like a cross between a redwood tree and a jungle gym, is being hoisted into place with a block and tackle. If it should slip or collapse, if the rope holding it should part, the whole thing would come crashing down on the tight-packed crowd of teenyboppers, Moraga merchants, heads, suburban housewives, Berkeley street people, speed freaks, Sunday drivers, hikers, joggers, weekend hippies, nature nuts, and rock musicians. Even if there was a warning, they wouldn't hear it. They are surrounded by rock groups in the process of warming up, caught in a crossfire of amplified *booms, eeks, yawps.*

"I was stoned on acid," says a man who was there that day, "and I was terrified that something was going to happen, that the ropes would break and children would be crushed or something."

Digging in, muscle against weight, the gang of men on the

rope gently, *gently* lowers the huge, spidery thing until it rests beam against beam against earth. The angles and cuts that took three days to figure out work. Tension. Compression. Balance. Before the block and tackle are even disconnected, children are scrambling up into it, turning it into a monkey house. The first of the groups has set up in front of it and now begins to play, amplified lead guitars, amplified bass guitars, amplified voices smothering the sound of the band's own gasoline-generated power, booming up, over the school and through the trees to homes along the hillside, where people shut windows, doors, *anything* to keep it out. As if the miles of parked cars and roving bands of teenyboppers weren't nuisance enough. It's like Poe's Red Death.

All to raise money for the store. A benefit in August of 1967, two full years before Woodstock, with some of the groups from San Francisco and Berkeley: Country Joe and the Fish and The Grateful Dead and the others. Canyon's young people had friends in the groups and had persuaded them to come. Everything was to be properly organized. Apply to the county for permits. Collect fees on the road. Truck in portable toilets. Run a shuttle service from Moraga for hitchhikers. Clean up all debris. They'd promoted it in underground papers like *The Berkeley Barb* and planned the dome as a sort of monument to Canyon's way of doing things, of turning obstacles into achievement.

There was a good response from the groups; more musicians than they needed were willing to come and play. There were articles in the underground press and ads in the suburban papers. Every teen-ager in Moraga and Orinda seemed to know about the Happening. Yet nobody really knew what to expect. How big a crowd would there really be? What would it do to Canyon?

Then, on the day before the benefit, the county permits were denied. They wouldn't be allowed to have cars parking along miles of county road or to collect fees. Everything had fallen through. Yet it was too late. The ads were out. The groups were coming. People could not be discouraged or turned away. A last-minute attempt to reach the President of the Board of Supervisors failed. He was unavailable. There was nothing to do but to go through with it.

In the town of Moraga alarmed homeowners stared at the unfamiliar cars parked in front of their houses and at the groups of costumed, psychedelic-looking children standing on corners, waiting for flower-painted Volkswagen buses or pickup trucks to haul them to whatever was going on in Canyon.

Pinehurst Road, where there are no houses or gas stations, only East Bay MUD's fenced-off watershed lands, was bumper to bumper with parked cars, as though some mammoth football game were being played out in the redwoods.

The crowd around the school was in the thousands, spilling over the grove and into the schoolyard, beyond the schoolyard and into the larger grove down the creek. Groups of young people, many of them in bizarre outfits, were wandering along the railroad bed or sitting on the cement retaining wall of the bridge or squatting down beside the creek. The thing about this music, you don't have to watch it to listen to it. It was everywhere. And so were the people who came to hear it. Packed into noisy cars roaring up and down the Redwood Highway, strolling along the paths, nodding approvingly at the homes in the trees, standing around in a group by the store, hairy, atavistic, threatening-looking.

The music and the traffic along the road and the shuttle service to Moraga continued until two o'clock in the morning, to the further annoyance of people for whom the whole experience had been a bad odor to be endured, but not ignored. There would be letters and formal complaints to the Board of Supervisors, but those were to be expected.

In the cold light of the foggy morning after, the grove and the schoolyard are a garbage dump, and the roadside is littered with debris. But this, too, has been taken into account. Later in the day a man from the Sewage Department, one of the younger ones, comes out to make an inspection of the store. He had been out to the benefit the day before and is aware of the size of the crowd. The cleanup, he says, is incredible.

The younger members of the community, gathering as planned, have collected the papers and cans and discarded food and cleaned and raked the grove. Then, moving out, carrying burlap sacks, they have followed the road, picking up every bit of litter and trash for two miles in both directions. Canyon now looks just as it did before the Happening, with one exception: the geodesic dome filling a corner of the schoolyard. And that already meets the community definition of appropriateness. It looks as if it grew there.

Awakening to the full impact of their monumental bender, the people of Canyon now discovered that their community had moved from the quiet wings of life in Contra Costa County to stage center. The noise, crowds, and publicity associated with the event had made "Canyon" locally synonymous with "hippie," and the trickle of visitors from Berkeley was diluted by a regular weekend stream of children from the orderly, upper-middle-class communities nearby (Orinda, Moraga, Walnut Creek) who saw in Canyon everything they felt they lacked at home. Dirt roads and paths with people walking on them, instead of just cars passing by. People who smiled or waved or who would stop and talk to you, so you could lose the oppressive feeling of being the only person in the world. A place where people *gathered*, where it doesn't say PRIVATE PROPERTY all over everything, where every dog isn't tied up or on a leash, where there aren't any lawns and old mattresses leaking stuffing are left out under the trees and there are domes with no one in them, where you can camp out or build a fire without being arrested, get something to eat and maybe some grass, a place that, finally, you can run to when the hassling at home just gets to be too much.

They came every weekend, walking and talking and making

friends, and some of them learned how to provide for themselves, how to find water and dispose of waste, how to cook outdoors and build with materials that are light or natural or cheap. They were the ones who really seemed to have caught on to what Canyon was all about. Others, confusing freedom with license, uncertain just what civilized ways one discards in a wilderness or eager to express hostility toward any kind of social regulation, left trash and litter strewn along the paths, lit fires, broke windows, committed petty thefts and hung around the store, getting in people's way and hurling insults at older residents. They lingered like sores on the community, and to people driving by on Pinehurst Road these became Canyon's most identifiable inhabitants. Idle flower children. Teenyboppers. Hippies.

Nobody in Canyon really knew what to do about them, especially the ones who came to stay.

"After all," says a man who has lived in the community for more than twenty years, "kids weren't running away from Canyon. They were running away from other communities and coming here. We don't know how we can be blamed for that."

Yet, once there, people did feel responsible for them. Someone knocks at your door in the middle of the night, miles from any town, asking for food or a place to sleep, and what are you supposed to do, turn him away? So you let him sleep in your dome or your tree house or in the junked car up at the top of the road. You feed him and show him a few things and try to keep an eye on him so he doesn't get hurt or set the hillside on fire, and maybe talk to him a little about going back, only you don't push it, because how are you to know what it is he's running away from? And, above all, you don't call the cops. And in a few days or maybe a couple of weeks he's gone, moved on or moved home. Except in a few cases, those rare instances when a kid's hair will begin to get long and you'll notice him walking in the woods looking at things, at ease there, barefoot maybe, walking on the earth in that light way that shows he really feels it, the way city people never can. And then one day when you're working he comes up to you, Indian-quiet, and asks if you'd mind if he put up a place of his own over by the madrone tree or between the live oaks, and you know he's here to stay for as long as he can get away with it. And you tell him sure, of course, and offer to lend him your tools.

Michael was one of the ones who came to Canyon that way. He'd run away from the county juvenile home, where he'd been held on a pot charge, and had come to Canyon and hidden out for over a month. A woman in the community gave him a place to sleep and some food, and the other people had got to know him and like him as he found the feel of the place. A nice kid, who'd been screwed up, yes, but who was coming around.

Then Michael's mother found out that Michael was in Canyon, and instead of coming out after him herself, she went to the police and they came out to get him. When she saw her son, she began bawling him out, right there in front of everybody, in front of the police with their guns and in front of the people who lived in the community and in front of the Canyon woman who'd fed Michael and given him a place to stay. Michael's mother slapped him and pulled his hair and said the people watching were not fit to be members of the human race. Michael was going back to the juvenile home where he belonged. At this, the woman who'd been looking after Michael yelled to him, urging him to run. Michael took off, a cop started after him, and the woman started scuffling with the cop. Michael was caught and cuffed and led away, back to his two homes, juvenile and legal, and away from the only home he wanted. The woman who had sheltered him was then cited for assaulting an officer and was prosecuted by the Contra Costa District Attorney. A jury acquitted her by a narrow margin. After this the county began proceedings to take her year-old child away from her. This action was dropped when it was discovered that she owned a home in Berkeley and lived in Canyon out of personal preference. It had been assumed that she was motivated by poverty or depravity.

These and other events in Canyon were treated in the suburban press, with the notable exception of the Contra Costa *Times*, as "hippie happenings," and the community was characterized as the county's Haight-Ashbury. One paper ran a photographic essay depicting Canyon's radical architecture, junked cars, and litter, accompanied by the unctuous kind of copy peculiar to the Modern Living sections of Sunday newspapers: "Spacious, elegant and airy, a place to be at home with the great outdoors." Beneath the facetious surface of the piece was the implicit message that this portrait of shacks, wrecks, and litter typified Canyon life generally and that the people who chose to live this way were parasitic vagrants and therefore fair game. Moreover, it was done with an insensitivity that the same paper would never have displayed toward either a conventional suburban community or an urban ghetto, and demonstrated Canyon's lack of real economic or political power.

These incidents and articles were all that most people in Contra Costa County knew about Canyon, and all that many of them needed to know. For people upset at the county's growing drug and runaway problems, bewildered by the attitudes and dress of the young, or angry at opposition to the Vietnam War, Canyon was a contaminant, the source of many sicknesses. Where before, individuals in the Health Department and the management of East Bay MUD had objected to the community because it was where it was, opposition now broadened to include church groups, homeowners in the neighboring communities, real-estate men, parents of teen-age children, and public officials like the Supervisor who privately admitted he was going to "get Canyon," who were against the community because of the people who lived there.

If you were young and you lived in Canyon, just going to the store to buy food now meant crossing over into an alien and often hostile culture, where long hair and dusty feet were barely tolerated, and where the simple matter of cashing a check could provoke a public inquisition into your place and length of employment and residence—an inquisition whose purpose was, at least in part, to embarrass you and discourage your trade.

Because the county had denied the necessary permits, the stock of the rebuilt Canyon Store was confined to local handicrafts, newspapers, and ZigZag cigarette papers, and the nearest place to shop remained a large, gleaming shopping-center supermarket, where the two cultures met uneasily over the produce. When one young runaway, eventually ostracized from Canyon, took to shoplifting food and eating it openly in the store, scattering rinds and peels on the floor and yelling obscenities at suburban matrons, it was the whole community that had to take the blame.

Nine / Canyon Cinema

He sits at the wheel of a Dodge pickup truck, driving west on U.S. Alternate 90 from Houston, Texas, where he is conducting a film workshop at Rice University, to Austin, where he is giving a show that night. As he steers with one hand and occasionally with his knee ("This truck won't steer itself. With my Volkswagen I'd always steer with my knee and eat with one hand and run my tape recorder and my camera with my other"), passing through flat, beautiful, half-green, half-brown countryside under a clear, cold November sky, he munches grapes, eats yogurt, and belches occasionally, while speaking into a tape-recorder microphone about himself and Canyon and his life there, as southeast Texas slips along the horizon of the ears. The Brazos . . . Rosenberg . . . Eagle Lake . . .

"I made a few visits out to Canyon not long ago, seeing a few friends after a long time, and I said to them then that it seemed like there had been a revival of the community again, and it surprised me, because a number of revivals back before that I had given up on Canyon.

"I lived there first in about 1959, I think, in Mr. Leydickson's old house. I had been just living a nothing life, doing nothing in Berkeley, and one dark, very rainy night I went out there. I think the reason I went out there was because I heard there was a girl living there, and I thought she must be very special to be living out there by herself. I had been given explicit instructions on how to get there, so I got up on that old railroad bed. I parked and found my way in and very slowly made my way in the darkness above the stream bed and got to that little Japanese bridge that goes over to the house and up each one of those individually set stones up the path to the front, and I even went up on the porch and to that rounded sea-captain's window, but I didn't go in. I didn't feel like I belonged there or something. But there was this one light bulb burning inside, and I could see in, and it was the most mysterious house I had ever seen. Really dark, surrounded by trees, with a stained-glass window. That house is centered in one of my basic dreams ever since. Much like Jung's house that he fashioned for himself to represent his whole view of man and the universe, the conscious and the unconscious. Really, I'm constantly exploring some secret room in that house in dreams. Or taking people there or returning there and finding it winter and so on, a really kind of basic psychological vessel, that house was.

"So I went out there every day for a while and talked to Mr. Leydickson and tried to get him to rent it to me. Which was the way of people after me. All the time I was out there, there was always somebody trying to talk one of the few owners of a house into letting him live there. And finally he agreed to let me move in.

"So I lived up in that really dark house, all by myself with my dog, and then she had pups. And John, my neighbor, up the hill above me in the woods. There was no path going up there, not from my house, and I could hear him up there sometimes, singing. I used to work for him. Perfectly pleasant job, where we'd all get plenty of big, fat Italian sandwiches for lunch that he made. He had to advertise in the paper every so often for companionship. Such a variety of men would come out there to stay with him! Guys temporarily between this or that. Usually take advantage of him in one way or another. One was a kind of YMCA type, a young leader of boys, full of energy and a kind of fundamentalist, full of dogmatic ideas. I remember seeing him up early in the morning taking a vigorous outdoor shower and moving rapidly around the yard and chopping wood and talking about some lady friend who just didn't see his way, *the* way.

"Then along comes a man in a kind of black-and-gold flowing robe. He was a big man, with white skin and somewhat of a Yoga master, I believe, and very cruel. He had a great, huge, heavy chest with all his belongings, and very neatly lettered all around the chest was his name and date and serial number and all the places he had served when he was in the U.S. Army, and he made John carry the chest up to the house. He would lay around. Get up around eleven or noon. John would feed him, then John would go off to work. And he'd be there, wearing this huge black-and-gold silk robe. He loved guns, and all of us hated to have guns around in the canyon. And he just tortured us by firing off these guns all the time, grinning evilly. He used to come down and visit me, and I really didn't like having visitors, because I was always doing some kind of work.

"I used to spend a lot of time with some of the Asian students from Mills College. I had a Fiat, and I used to drive it into Mills, and we'd come out—three or four girls and I—and sit on the floor in front of a wood fire, and one of the girls would cook on a different evening this Chinese or Japanese food. Then I finally went off to England and gave up the house.

"When I came back, I moved up in the other end of Canyon, up high, near the crossroads. I was living with Kikuku at the time, and we had a really good life. And David was living up on the hill with Katy. We had an old TV that someone had given us, and it barely worked, and David was an avid television watcher, so we used to watch all the westerns. Lay out a blanket and Kikuku would bring in some food and all of us would lie and watch TV. And it was a very beautiful spring, long, tall grass, and I started my first film there. And then we got the idea of beginning Canyon Cinema, since I could see that there was absolutely no way to distribute films that I was going to make and, it seemed, that others were going to be making.

"And so I was making *On Sundays*, a film of Miss Wong, a friend of mine and my dogs, just beginning to very slowly learn how to make films. I bought a good projector, finally, on time payments; we got a cheap surplus screen and stretched it out on a framework on the hill behind one of Mr. Johnson's old houses. Then we kind of looked around the top of Canyon and found that there were a lot of old park benches that had been there for years, a few benches over in the old, abandoned church, and we would take them over there every Friday or Saturday night—or maybe it was Sundays—and the kids would come down and set up the theater. Kikuku would be making popcorn, and the kids would be setting up the benches, the screen would be up there permanently on the hill, and I'd set up the projector inside the kitchen, with the speaker outside on the hill. And then everybody would come, and I started this thing called Canyon Cinema. The shows would be mostly those free Embassy films, since hardly anybody was making his own films at the time, and the only other films were for rentals that we couldn't afford. And I'd make little simple things up on the hill, like David making a huge sculpture. Things like that. Also, I initiated an extensive correspondence into all kinds of things that concerned film and finally got stationery when I moved into Berkeley, but at the time I was also sending postcards around in the Bay Area announcing each week's show.

"It became a really full-time life right away, programming and making my own films and taking care of the house, trying to keep one of the cars running. We put a light bulb up in our garage down by the road below the house and a sign that said CANYON CINEMA. So that's how the name began. And we'd announce the coming show on the bulletin board down by the

Canyon

post office and store, but the rsepectable Canyon residents always resisted the idea—just as people do in all the towns in the United States—any kind of a new thing coming in. There was a constant resistance there—and threat—and that's why, as I say, I never gave much hope of there being a community there, of any kind.

"I remember nearly having a fight with Mr. Whatchama-diddy, the Swedish carpenter up on the hill. I don't know what's become of him. He was a great big powerful man, drove home every day from work, and my dog would chase his car because he brought his dog along. And he would just get in a rage. And he came out after my dog with an iron pipe one day, and I was barefoot. I was sitting up on one of my porches, I remember. I jumped off instantly and was down on that road in a flash and told him if he made another move, I'd kill him, right on the spot.

"The poor guy thought somebody was really going to kill him, I guess. He was *two* of me. But he went directly home and called the sheriff, and the sheriff came out that evening, and I was out, and poor Kikuku she said, "Oh, I'm sure he didn't mean that." She was really an exceptional woman. So we went through all those silly conflicts I've found everywhere I've gone, anywhere I've had a house since.

"Meanwhile, we really developed Canyon Cinema, and gradually we had a full house every week. The kids would sit up on the roof of the house. I remember showing Michael Putnam's first film about a stripper in San Francisco. We gave a premiere of that film and then a premiere of my film, *On Sundays*, at our theater, as well as some shorter works.

"All this time I'd been taking small jobs, working for Canyon Construction once in a while or whatever, trying to keep unemployment going from a job I'd had. I remember I had a job at Safeway, but I was fired there. It was in Richmond. The manager lived in a glass cage up above all the workers in the store and watched down on us like an owl. He was a very nervous man,

68

and one evening he had me into his cage, and he says, 'I don't think the food game is your line. I hate to do this to a married man (I'd told him I was married to get the job), but we're going to have to let you go.' And I was so relieved, and I had to look a little perturbed and a little bit lost and so on, but that was really a relief, and so I got twenty dollars a week after that or something, and all that went into film—I mean every single, solitary ha'penny—for years.

"In my own work I'd gradually take out loans at banks and accumulate one necessary piece of equipment at a time, over the years, and try to borrow or rent whatever else I needed. Most of my films were made that way until recently.

"We had free wine sometimes, free popcorn, people wandering around in the night. It was a monstrous amount of work.

"Then Chickie Strand invented the *Canyon Cinema News* as a monthly sheet of information, a journal, since there really started to be an American film movement, and now it's very important in the film world. And that was quite a chore to keep that coming out every month, and still is.

"We invented our own thing and nurtured it, and it developed, it lived, it continued for quite a few years and still, in its present shape, continues. And it began in a very happy time with myself and Kikuku living in that house up on the hill, taking random movie film of the kids and the things in Canyon and showing it of an evening. Both David and I had good ladies, and the grass was really tall that year."

Ten / To the Edge

Driving up the Redwood Highway at night in the late 1960's, going slowly over the bumps and carefully around the curves, you never knew what your headlights might fall upon. A carload of kids drinking or smoking dope. A man standing beside a fire, naked. A couple making out. Obscene words painted on a junked, gutted car. A motorcycle roaring at you down the center of the road. Part of your fence knocked down and your garden torn up by dogs. And the noises. Weird, animallike calls and cries at all hours and eerie, monotonous Eastern music. And the racket from those happenings in the grove. Outrageous. It sounded as if it was coming from the next room and made it impossible to concentrate on anything. But what was a person to do in such situations, walk up to some stranger in the dark and tell him to put his fire out and his clothes on? God knows what he might be smoking or swallowing or shooting into himself. No, the sensible thing was to ignore all of this as best you could, to pretend these things didn't exist and to hope that they would go away, and if they didn't, then to call in the police. But if you had lived in Canyon for more than twenty years, as more than ten families had, you couldn't help feeling that there was something fundamental missing among these young people, a respect for others that once had made it possible to go wherever you pleased in perfect safety. Now there were places in Canyon where you didn't go even in daylight, and you had the feeling that you were a stranger in your own community.

Within Canyon, young and old now lived in an almost constant state of tension. Everyone was on edge, and the smallest annoyances—a car parked in someone else's way, litter, a noisy party—were frequently taken as direct insults. To the older members of the community the Happening had been a declaration of war, and the influx of hippies and teenyboppers that followed it an invasion that was turning Canyon into a combination auto junk yard, garbage dump, and juvenile home. While to the young, the older people were narrow-minded, prejudiced, selfish, and uptight.

It did little good for some of the young people to explain that they, too, were upset at the litter and the influx of transients, that they had been victimized by burglaries and vandalism, and that they feared fires as much as the older residents did. The fact remained that before *they* came, none of these nuisances existed.

"I'm sorry I didn't live here twenty years ago," says a young Canyon man in mock apology. "But my mother wouldn't let me cross the street."

When SuperJoel, trying to make amends to the community for a multitude of earlier offenses, stopped a carload of youngsters on the Redwood Highway who had been drinking on the ridge and told them it was a private road and if they wanted to drink they ought to do their drinking elsewhere, one of the older residents immediately rushed out of his house and hotly contradicted him. This was *not* a private road; it was a *public* road, open to anybody. Forget the trespassing. Forget the drinking. He took their side because SuperJoel had taken the other.

Years before, a local woman had summed up the animating

spirit of Canyon: "It's a village where everybody knows what everybody else is doing, but nobody cares."

Now the woman who had said that had moved away, and in Canyon everybody seemed obsessed by what his neighbor was or wasn't doing. Instead of continuing to dissent from outside society in the manner the older people had, the new residents insisted on going further, on exploring new alternatives, on living in ways that seemed to challenge the assumptions on which life in Canyon itself had always been based. The sense of limits, of an unwritten community code of restraint on individualistic behavior, seemed to have disappeared, and with it the coercive power of neighbors' disapproval.

There was a young woman, well educated like the people who had lived in Canyon before, pretty, always neatly dressed, who had been living with a wild-looking young man up near the top of the ridge. Together, they had built a large geodesic dome, made of thirty sheets of plywood curved and bolted together, with cut-out pentagonals for windows, on a brushy slope overlooking the community. Then another young man, a friend of the first man, moved into Canyon, met the young woman, and married her in a pastoral ceremony in a local meadow. The young woman and her husband then chose a site, built a foundation of concrete pilings and on it a deck of wood and brick, and set on the deck the dome that the girl had built with the first man. The couple piped in water from a spring, installed a gasoline-powered generator to run power tools, built an access road, brought in a tank trailer for butane gas, a refrigerator, stove, and hot-water heater, plus a battery-operated radio and TV.

The house was just up the road from where the girl had been living before; she and the two men were partners in the same land-ownership association; there was no denial or concealment of the previous arrangement, and the three seemed to have remained neighbors and friends. Apparently none of this bothered the people involved at all, but to a few of the older residents the unusual relationship, the fact that the construction was done without a building permit, and the bunkerlike permanence of the building itself seemed both defiant and, somehow, licentious.

The young woman, whose wholesome prettiness combined with her restless energy, intelligence, and iron will seem to beg and command attention at the same time, soon became symbol and spokeswoman for the new Canyon, the sort of personality, strong and photogenic, that reporters find it difficult to ignore. The classic Nice, Intelligent Young Woman, she seemed to be the walking refutation of all the bad things people were saying about the younger residents of Canyon. Hippies were dirty, apathetic, strung-out, social rejects. She was well groomed, obviously healthy, vital, and a former debutante. Whenever there was a newspaper article about the community, she would be the individual quoted. Or, in a television interview, hers would be the face upon the screen. For some of the older women in the community she became a kind of female Dorian Gray, sinister in her very youth and attractiveness, and she was referred to on the straight side of Canyon resentfully as the Hippie Queen.

Down the slope below the dome house, where the foliage of the trees begins to merge and shut out the sun and there are only winding footpaths between neighbors, was another controversial house, of concern to people in Canyon less because of the man who lived there than because of what he lived *on*.

Starting with what had been just a wide spot in a hillside path, the man, lean, big-eyed, with long brown hair and a gentle but determined manner, had built a retaining wall out of logs trimmed from existing trees ("All I do is prune the forest. Look —you can see where it's been cleared") and created his own lot from garbage, scraps, human waste, and dirt fill, above which he lived in a one-room cabin. The house and grounds were undeniably tidy, the amounts of waste were small, and there was no odor. But as the land around his house expanded, his neighbors

73

couldn't help wondering about—and worrying about—the possibility of rats and the risks of disease.

Another man had incorporated into the remodeling of an existing house the junked hulks of three old automobiles, rust-streaked, windowless, wheels removed, and apparently a permanent fixture of the local landscape. He also kept another four or five old cars parked nearby, in the process of either mechanical restoration or conversion into construction material, making the scene around his house—at the border between the old Canyon and the new—resemble the infield at an automobile destruction derby.

But most inexplicable of all was the young man who insisted, as a means of personal expression, upon painting his name in large letters on any sort of sizable debris—most frequently, abandoned cars—standing about in the community. He made no attempt to hide his identity. Rather he saw it as his message, and graffiti as his medium. Apparently, feeling his style had developed sufficiently, he had, by the spring of 1971, begun holding his first show on the wooden construction hoardings of downtown San Francisco.

Values such as these proved untranslatable into the currency of an older Canyon. It was one thing to tolerate a neighbor's individual peculiarities. It was another to watch him flaunt them. The new people roamed the community without guilt, smiled and waved to people they had offended, invited their seething neighbors to their noisy parties, and seemed intent on establishing an anarchistic rule of exceptions. The people whose behavior seemed extreme were not only accepted by their peers, the other Canyon young, but were frequently admired; some of them were among the young community's leaders. Only at the behavior of SuperJoel did young and old in Canyon all seem to draw the line. His antics—like standing at the bottom of the road one night and screaming up at the houses on the hill, "Acid! Acid! Acid!"—began to seem defamatory and belligerent to everyone. Although, in putting down SuperJoel there was an element of elevating oneself, of becoming respectable by comparison.

For it was a fact that on that same hillside almost every night most of the households were turning on. Particularly the ones without electricity.

Yet, at bottom, the people in Canyon, young and old, were actually very much alike. Each person was an individual who disliked rules and being told what to do. The older residents had broken away from the society of their day and built a community in their own style, renovating old houses, constructing a road, forming a Community Club. Now a new element had moved in, people who wanted to explore new modes of living, new kinds of architecture, new ways of appearance and dress, new relationships between people. And they insisted on doing things in their own way just as strongly as the earlier residents had.

The things the people of the old Canyon couldn't understand about the people of the new—their burning desire to own land, their belief in its independent power, the feeling that once a man owned property what he did with it was entirely his own business, the idea that though there are others around a person there is really nobody else who *is* him, who can think and do for him as he would think and do for himself, the conclusion that power delegated is power weakened and compromised—these pioneer-style notions were really things that they had never understood about themselves; and represented attitudes that had come to Canyon not with the new beards and longhairs, but with the old ones, the lumbermen and land grabbers who had first moved into The Redwoods more than a century before.

Throughout the summer of 1967 and the summer of 1968, the parasitic teenyboppers and runaways for whom the new Canyon was host continued to come out—loitering, camping, intruding, changing the face of the community, increasing the risks of fire. Early that second summer the County Agriculture Department, intending to create greater visibility along the main road, sprayed the weeds and brush on both sides of Pinehurst Road with desiccant, leaving a path of dead, dry vegetation passing through the community like a powder trail. Alarmed, residents asked the Sheriff's Department for some sort of regular fire patrol of the area, since it was, after all, a county road. But the patrols proved to be infrequent and inadequate. Instead, Canyon's fire patrol turned out to be a few of the more conscientious older residents and a few of the younger ones, who, when they saw people camping down by the grove, would approach quietly and ask them to please put their fires out. As a community service, performed without the authority of signs or badges or guns, it was not without its dangers. There were threats and minor scuffles, and once two angry drunks burned up the old wooden bridge that spanned the creek behind the school.

Each week seemed to produce a new incident, some new indignity to add to the list of offenses, as though a new set of values was spreading, funguslike, through the redwoods. Old residents whose children were enrolled in the Canyon School found their sons' and daughters' curiosity aroused by what they saw as the most unsavory of the new people, and feared that the children would be drawn under their influence. And people with friends elsewhere in the county discovered that the community which had been their pride had become an embarrassment. They were living in a nest of hippies, drug users, and runaways —a rural slum. You never knew what your friends outside Canyon might read. Or worse, what your visitors might see.

The tragic fact was that in a community which had always depended on individual give-and-take to resolve its grievances there were now people who refused to speak to one another, who preferred calling in outside authorities to deal with differences between themselves and their neighbors rather than discussing them face to face. In this respect, this atmosphere of distrust and misunderstanding, both young and old in Canyon were now living the life of the modern city dweller, which both groups professed to despise.

Eleven / Vigil

☆ Somehow, the two young, long-haired men had acquired some gray paint that was perfect. It was *the* official-looking Navy gray—battleship gray, admiral's staff-car gray, the exact shade— and they were spreading it very deliberately and very carefully on the old pickup truck. Fenders, hood, cab, bed. It was a strange sight when you thought about it. Here were these two, all long hair and mustaches and beards, painting an old truck not in any psychedelic colors or flower pattern, but in the drabbest, most Establishment, most official-looking color imaginable, standing back and examining their work and making every effort to do an unstreaked, gleaming, professional job. ☆

The two men were part of one of the earliest and longest of the protests against the Vietnam War, a protest that continued for over two years, drew participants from all over the country, and served as a model for similar demonstrations elsewhere. A protest that was run from a house in Canyon.

It began in the summer of 1966 at the Contra Costa Naval Weapons Station in Port Chicago as a one-day demonstration against the use of napalm in Vietnam. At that time all Navy

77

napalm bombs destined for the Far East were being shipped through Port Chicago, and part of the napalm was being delivered in trucks that had to pass through one of the Station's two gates.

A man who lives in Canyon now and a man named Jim who lived in Canyon then started organizing, about two months in advance, what they thought would be a one-day protest. There was to be a rally in the city of Concord's Community Park on the day after Hiroshima Day, followed by a march to Port Chicago. They let the Navy know that they were going to be there, and, though the city of Concord didn't grant the parade permit, the demonstrators marched anyhow.

At the end of the march there were 400 to 500 people waiting at the Weapons Station gates for the napalm trucks to arrive. Only none were coming. Notified of the protest, the Navy had simply held up the shipments for the day.

When the protesters discovered that there'd be no trucks that day they began to talk the whole idea over among themselves. There they were, having organized the whole thing and taken the time and marched out. It ought to count for something. They knew the Navy couldn't shut off the trucks forever. In fact, they'd probably resume the shipments the next day. So about fifty or sixty people decided that they would stay until the trucks came. Someone went out and bought food. A *Chronicle* delivery-truck driver left papers, his lunch, and a bottle of milk. Then the remaining marchers made themselves as comfortable as possible and went to sleep by the side of the road.

☆ After painting the truck the exact, official-looking Navy gray they wanted, touching up the uneven spots and eliminating the streaks, the two young men got some black paint and a long, thin brush. And on the door of the truck, touching with the brush and then drawing back for a critical squint at the work, they carefully painted in official-looking block letters: FOR OFFICIAL USE ONLY. ☆

———

Redwood grove, Canyon, California

Not giant soccer balls, but a characteristic Canyon house, consisting of three geodesic domes joined together

County notices: Officialdom posts a warning on the tumble-down store and post office

Fait accompli: If people are still getting mail there, how can the county deny a permit for its reconstruction?

Building Material
needed for Sat-Sun, Mon-Tues,

★★★★★★★★

2×4's, 2×6's
1×8's, 1×4's 1×12s
16d nails
8d nails
tar paper
staples+staplers
glass
toilet, sink
paint thinner
linseed oil
plywood

FOOD

bread
salads
cakes
cookies
pies
paper plates
silverwar
bowls- Bee,
Wine coffee

← Resistance, 1967: Canyon residents, defying the county, join forces to rebuild without permits

Canyon store and post office as reconstructed by volunteer labor

Canyon store and post office two years later, the morning after the
gasoline-pipeline break and the holocaust

At about four thirty the following morning the trucks started arriving and the protesters stirred and began crossing the road with their picket signs. Near the white line that marks the end of the county and the beginning of Navy property, people lay down on the road in front of the trucks. The drivers yelled and swore at them, threatened to run over them, but instead stopped. Then Marine Corps security guards and county sheriff's deputies dragged the protesters across the white line and arrested them. By ten o'clock twenty-six people had been charged with trespassing, creating a nuisance, and blocking a public road, and the papers had picked up the story: NAPALM PICKETING. 26 ARRESTED. The Port Chicago Vigil was under way.

☆ Next, the two men drilled a number of holes in the roof of the pickup truck's cab, fitted it with the necessary bolts and wires, and installed a rotating yellow light—the kind usually seen on tow trucks or other semiofficial vehicles. Then they tested it. It spun. It flashed. It was beautiful. ☆

At this point in the Vietnam War, the bombing of the North still had widespread support among the public at large, and in Contra Costa County antiwar protest was generally equated with treason. On at least one occasion Port Chicago pickets who had been arrested were attacked and beaten by their fellow inmates in the County Work Camp and had to be removed for their own protection. And the demonstrators at the gates were regularly manhandled by Marine security guards in the presence of county sheriffs, one of whom said that "we are just going to keep letting them push the demonstrators off the county road."

But as soon as the protesters were bailed out, they would return to the picket line. An organization was formed in Berkeley to raise bail, and eventually the first of the people arrested were acquitted in Federal District Court, when the lawyer for the Vigil established that about half of the pickets had not been on Navy property at all and that the other half had been forced on against their will. Gradually the original marchers were replaced by people who had heard about the Vigil across the country and had come to Port Chicago to take part.

An unwritten understanding evolved for the care and feeding of these newcomers: you go out and stand vigil and you'll have food and a roof over your head. The roof was the one on Jim's house in Canyon, which had gradually become the staging area for the entire Vigil, and the food was whatever could be raised through donations. Day in and day out for more than two years, Jim fed and housed an endless line of pickets, who came from all over the United States, his boarders ranging in number from as few as nine to as many as thirty-five.

Originally, people stood vigil in eight-hour shifts, round the clock. Then it became eight to five for the rest of the Vigil's existence. Some of the people who stood vigil were lost and simply sat, completely quiet, not even talking to their fellow demonstrators. Some were obnoxious. Others were conscientious, talking to and debating with civilian employees working at the Weapons Station about the war and what they were doing, even talking to the truck drivers, most of whom owned their own rigs and very few of whom were friendly.

Frequently local people or sailors who had had too much to drink came by in cars to harass the protesters. They threw beer bottles, yellow paint, tires. Occasionally they would wade in and start throwing punches. Cars were burned, and there were, of course, regular patriotically inspired streams of verbal abuse.

☆ When the truck was finished, the two young men began a more delicate remodeling job, this time on themselves. They shaved off their beards and mustaches and cut their hair short. Then they went out and bought plastic hard hats and clean, creased work clothes, like the kind workingmen types wear in commercials for heavy-duty laundry detergents. They put on their outfits and looked at their pickup truck and themselves. Perfect. ☆

———

Vigil

By the time the Vigil had gone on for about two years, Jim had grown weary of living in a crowd. His house was a dormitory, his dining room a mess hall. A conscientious objector who had been sent to McNeil Island in World War Two, Jim eventually felt that he had suffered enough for his own convictions. Also, partly as a result of the Vigil, his personal life had become incredibly complicated. He was now dividing it between two households in Canyon, between two women and two sets of children, seven in one house and one in another.

☆ Everything was ready. As a final touch, the two young men mounted a large, official-looking sign on the back of their truck and drove to the United Technology Corporation plant in Redwood City, where the napalm carriers took on their cargo. And when a loaded truck came out of the plant, they followed it in their Navy-gray pickup, with the flashing yellow light on the roof and FOR OFFICIAL USE ONLY neatly lettered on the side, with their clean-shaven faces and their hard hats and pressed work clothes. They followed trucks regularly from Redwood City all the way to Port Chicago. Up the Bayshore Freeway, across the bridge, along the Nimitz Freeway, in this official-looking truck carrying the sign USE EXTREME CAUTION—NAPALM BOMBS AHEAD. It did strange things to people along the highway and had an awful lot to do with the United Technology napalm operation being shut down. ☆

The raid on the Vigil House, when Jim was busted for possession of narcotics, was brutal. The house was raided by sheriff's deputies and narcotics agents, who found marijuana and LSD, which Canyon people insist was planted.

"Everybody knew the Vigil House was going to be raided," says a Canyon man who took part in the Vigil. "Nobody would have been dumb enough to leave any grass around there."

Twenty people were arrested in all, including a couple of teenage runaways, so Jim was charged with contributing to the delinquency of a minor as well as possession of narcotics, a felony and a misdemeanor at the same time. He was convicted and given three years' probation.

Shortly afterward, a young black man, a resident of Canyon, was arrested in San Diego and charged with smuggling narcotics. He was a friend of Jim's and was carrying one of Jim's credit cards. The county now charged Jim with conspiracy and threatened to revoke his probation. Jim would have to go back to jail, but he was fifty-two years old, and he said he simply couldn't. Instead, he turned the leadership of the Vigil over to people outside the community and sold his house; and the headquarters, dormitory, and mess hall for the Port Chicago Vigil moved away from Canyon.

Jim took his children and fled to Costa Rica, where he's living now. According to friends of his in Canyon, he doesn't like it much there.

Twelve / Water Brothers

It was Jim—the same Jim who had led the Port Chicago Peace Vigil and had gone to jail as a conscientious objector in World War Two—who had really organized the purchase of the Canyon Store. About twelve or thirteen years before, back when nobody had ever heard of communes, he had lived out of the country in a commune of some kind, and he used the tactical skills he had learned earlier to show his neighbors in Canyon exactly why and how the community should be saved. The Store Trust had been his idea, and in going around the community and talking to people, trying to raise the $14,000, he made everybody see what was going to have to be done in order to keep the community together, to keep the school open, to keep young families from moving away. Even people who disagreed with him politically had to respect his dedication to Canyon and his appetite for hard work. So they listened, and what Jim said made sense to some of the older people and to most of the young ones. The tide could be turned against the utilities district, providing people in Canyon stuck together, worked at raising money or finding interested buyers when land became available, were willing to go to court, and, above all, kept a close watch on the management and Board of Directors of East Bay MUD.

Though in theory Directors of East Bay MUD are elected by the people of the district they serve, actually no one has ever been elected to the Board. Each Director legally represents the entire three-county utilities district and runs for office in district-wide elections, usually appearing last on the ballot for a simple yes or no vote. Opposition on this basis is so costly that, in practice, Directors are appointed, then re-elected until they retire or die. As a result, it has been all but impossible to get new blood on the Board. East Bay MUD's water is excellent, service is good and the rates are reasonable; but the company has not been politically sensitive to the public it serves.

California state law, however, requires that any expenditures by a utility company must be approved by its board of directors. In effect, this means that the agenda of East Bay MUD's Board provides the only reliable public record of the company's activities and intentions. In the interests of self-preservation, people in Canyon made it the subject of close and regular study.

One day, not long after the acquisition of the Canyon Store, Jim noticed in a copy of the Board's agenda an item authorizing the purchase of property "in San Leandro." This might have meant the nearby city of San Leandro, but, assuming the worst, Jim decided it was probably the watershed area of the Upper San Leandro Reservoir and San Leandro Creek. Inquiring around the community, he learned that Mrs. Holmes, an old resident who owned twenty-six acres in Canyon, including six houses, five of which she rented out, had indeed put her property up for sale. Her house was at the crossroads at the top of the ridge, and Jim went to her nearest tenant, a young man who lived next door to Mrs. Holmes, and told him what he'd seen on the Board's agenda. The young man went to see his landlady.

Yes, Mrs. Holmes said, her property had been sold. She had signed an agreement with a real-estate agent acting in behalf of a land buyer for the utilities district. She had done so with regret, but East Bay MUD had offered her $55,000, and she knew no one in Canyon had that kind of money. The young man told her that the agreement she had signed might not have been final and that there might be a possibility of a counteroffer. Then he called a lawyer he knew, who said he didn't think the signed agreement was legally binding. The young man told Mrs. Holmes this and, cold with sweat, offered her $60,000, which he vowed he would raise, and Mrs. Holmes accepted. At the time the man didn't have a regular job.

When utilities-district officials learned that Mrs. Holmes intended to sell to people in Canyon, they sent their land buyer out to her house, accompanied by the real-estate agent, and these two men personally threatened to sue her for violating the agreement. Mrs. Holmes insisted that she was going to give her neighbors one month to come up with the money, and eventually the utilities district withdrew the threat, perhaps recognizing the difficulty that Canyon people would have raising such a sum in a limited time.

This time it was the young element of the community scrounging and hustling and trying to put together an organization, but with their own methods and in their own style. The Canyon people who had organized the Store Trust had used their own property as a base and had been able to raise the final $4,000 with a bank loan. The new group, however, owned almost no land or houses and had no prospects of bank assistance. They would have to put up either their own cash, or whatever they could raise without collateral.

Some of them had recently been reading the Robert Heinlein novel *Stranger in a Strange Land,* in which people, by the act of sharing water, symbolically become water brothers, sharing all. They decided to form an association and call it, after the book, the Water Brothers. The man who lived next door to Mrs. Holmes knew a girl who worked at a San Francisco television station, and she arranged for a news team to be sent out for an interview in which he gave his version of what was going on in

Canyon. The Water Brothers also placed a series of ads in *The Berkeley Barb* inviting people to buy into the association, and *The Barb* ran some articles about Canyon. It wasn't long before people began to get interested and the contributions started coming in.

The Canyon Water Brothers became a legal entity on September 20, 1967, an association with a written constitution. Membership is limited to sixteen shareowners, and a minimum contribution of $5,000 is required of everyone. For this share a member gets to choose his homesite from the available acreage, with people making the largest or earliest contributions getting first choice. A capital account is maintained to show initial contributions, title is in the name of the Water Brothers, and the association owns and operates five common buildings and has the first option to repurchase membership.

From the beginning it was agreed that the Water Brothers would not refuse anybody, that membership would be on a first-come, first-served basis, whether the people who came were friends of people already in the community or not. Those who did come were served a rather mixed prospect: raw land surrounded by beautiful trees and some spectacular views, but without water, electricity, sewerage, or access roads. There were the five old houses, where some rental space was available, but the possibility of doing any building on your chosen site was dimmed by a county moratorium on septic tanks and by the fact that it was still all but impossible to get a permit to build a new building in Canyon. The Water Brothers had discussed formation of their own sewer district with a man from the county's Local Agency Formation Commission, but the official reaction was vague and indefinite and rested on a sort of gentlemen's agreement not to post the existing houses. What you actually got for a $5000-minimum investment in the Water Brothers was an unimproved homesite on which you weren't legally allowed to build anything, the possibility of renting space in one of five run-down summer houses, and the chance to live in proximity to a bunch of people you hardly knew, in a community in danger of going under entirely. It wasn't really an investment at all but a declaration of faith.

Probably this was why the Water Brothers attracted the kind of people they did, people to whom the purchase of land in Canyon under such circumstances presented the challenge of putting themselves and their savings where their convictions were. If you were dissatisfied with the quality of contemporary American life and distressed at the direction in which it seemed to be heading, if you believed in the preservation of some sort of ecological balance and maximum individual freedom combined with dedicated community action, if you maintained in a practical as well as in an emotional way that indifference to human and natural values was actually an attack on them, then investment in Canyon and acceptance of its constant, common struggle amounted to the moral equivalent of enlistment in a war.

Through television and the classified graffiti of *The Barb*, the Water Brothers drew their extraordinary investors: a schoolteacher, a lawyer, a tax investigator for the government, a civil engineer with a Ph.D.—some of them complete strangers to Canyon and to the people who lived there. In this manner Mrs. Holmes's price was met in full and in cash, within the allotted time, and twenty-six more acres of Canyon land that East Bay MUD badly wanted remained in the hands of the community.

Though no particular plot of land went with each Water Brothers membership, the shareowners, in choosing their sites, tended to cluster around the top of the ridge, in the land close to the fire trail, where it is easiest to build. Actually, building was mostly confined to daydreams and sketches, since the shareowners couldn't get legal permission to do anything with their land beyond camping on it.

Unable to do as they wished with their land, the Water Brothers became a sort of core organization within the community, canvassing among their neighbors, spreading local political information, holding regular meetings, planning legal tactics and organizational strategy, forming a chorus of opinion perhaps more audible to officials at the county level. Periodically, individual Water Brothers shareowners applied for permits to build homes on their sites, and the permits were regularly denied for lack of sewage disposal. What building did go on in the acquired acreage was sporadic and experimental, domes and shacks, which were not used as residences except by occasional teen-age runaways.

With the founding of the association came the first set of formal property distinctions among the young people in Canyon. Now they were divided into landed people, homeowners, and Water Brothers on the one hand, and landless tenants or squatters on the other. Although the people outside the association valued the impetus it gave to Canyon's interests, they distrusted it for being restricted, a group of people linked by money and legal title instead of by common feelings and ideas, a community within a community.

Sharing common land, common houses, and a consensus of forethought, the people in the Water Brothers tended to cling together, to share the older houses as living quarters, to visit back and forth, to run errands and buy materials together, to look after one another's houses and children, and to confide in one another. This produced among some of the young people outside the association feelings of exclusion and resentment.

"I'm not into the Water Brothers thing," says a solitary Canyon man, recognizing in membership a transition to another set of values.

The Water Brothers were landowners now, bound to a certain primary group of people and a certain plot of ground, and beneath the personal relationships among themselves and with the other young people, there was an undercurrent, a lingering ethical quandary. Were they primarily property owners like the older people of Canyon, or were they really some new breed of communalists?

When a temporary shack, built by someone who wasn't a

member of the association, was found on Water Brothers land, the ethical quandary took physical form. What was to be done? A member of the association, in an act that some of the Brothers deplore but most of them conveniently forget, resolved the issue, at least for himself. He tore the shack down. It was the last attempt by an outsider to build on Water Brothers land.

Thirteen / Wobbly

The founder of the Canyon Water Brothers is a tall, soft-spoken young man, with a slow-moving, commanding physical presence. He looks like the sole survivor of a cartoon shipwreck—shoulder-length hair, untrimmed beard, no shirt or shoes, ragged, cutoff Levis for pants —who, as though having made his way inland and improvised a shelter out of available materials, is living in as self-sufficient a manner as possible off the land.

But this is no ordinary castaway. Rather, he is an oceanless Robinson Crusoe, intelligent and accomplished, who has re-made his corner of the world, which happens to be at the residential crossroads of Canyon and on the border between the old residents and the new, according to his own principles. But he is a Crusoe without privacy. His house, a hyperbolic paraboloid form (peaked roof of eucalyptus poles complete with leaves, conical-shaped sides with the side facing west left open to the trees, sky, and rain), allows the sounds and odors of Canyon— arguing voices, music, bird cries, burning grass, chants, patchouli oil, a trumpet scale, a revving motorcycle engine—to flow through it like air. There are no locks, windows, or doors. Anyone walking by on the road above can eavesdrop on his life, observe him tinkering at the large workbench beside his entrance, or call down to him for a drink of water, which he'll let you draw from the strange, convoluted faucet—pipe joint added upon pipe joint—above his sink. He is as exposed as his house. His parties are enthusiastically regarded as the best in Canyon, yet his private life remains intact. It seems to spill outward like lava, absorbing everything it comes in contact with, then cooling into stone, an unconcealed fact of the landscape, requiring no protection of its own.

"Funny thing," says an older resident who knows and likes him, "when we had the trouble with the authorities and the postings, his house was the older people's main target—and he got off scot-free."

Though he negotiated the land purchase on which the Water Brothers is based, he seems detached from the association, and somewhat wary of it.

"Personally, I don't want to see an individual lose initiative because of participating in a co-operative venture. What you do with your land is your own business. I hope we don't get rigid and institutionalized."

He is candid and guileless, drawing sustenance from wellsprings of his own. When no one else in Canyon would put up with SuperJoel, he took him in, then finally threw him out. ("He threw my cat out, so I threw him out.") The open side of his house makes it miserable here, he admits, about one month out of the year during Canyon's annual heavy rain. But he feels it's not worth shutting himself in the rest of the year because of that. An anarchist, he is a member of the International Workers of the World.

"After I felt Cal Poly, where I'd been studying aeronautical engineering, I was living in Berkeley and working for Standard Oil. Fidel Castro had come to power in Cuba, and I started to organize a group of students who wanted to go down there. We tried to keep things as quiet as possible because of the travel ban. Some people were in it for political and business purposes, and I resented that, but I went anyway. We traveled by Volkswagen to Mexico City, where there was some difficulty about getting visas, and the trip fell through. But in the course of this attempted trip I got involved with a family who lived in Canyon.

"After that I moved to Big Sur, where I lived in a small house that overlooked the sea. It had only three walls, nothing on the sea side but the sun and the ocean and the stars. It was summer, so the weather was no problem. A friend of mine [the man who now heads Canyon Construction] was trying to build a business, marketing organically raised vegetables, but he had a wild reputation and was refused a business license to sell his produce by the health authorities. In order to get ready for winter I began gathering driftwood on the beaches nearby. I was rousted by the San Luis Obispo county sheriffs while collecting wood on the beach. I had heard about Canyon from these people who had been involved in the Cuban thing. And now my friend, who was with me on the beach, moved to Canyon. After a while I moved here, too.

"I lived in a little Sheetrock-wall house and began putting in foundations and repairing things. I was working in the building trades at that time. I felt I was lacking a practical background—a basic feeling for materials and an understanding of how things are put together—and I wanted to continue my education.

"I became a carpenter, and I began to feel it was fulfilling a part of me that school wasn't. One of the early jobs I did was to build a bathroom for somebody in Berkeley. I made it out of tile, like a grotto, and a number of people expressed interest in my work and ideas.

"Then, along with some other Wobblies, I went to Mississippi to rebuild a church. We were all friends and were all in the construction trades, and the Quakers were paying our way. On the way, in Arizona, our group visited an idol of mine, Paolo Soleri, who uses earth in building forms. Soleri invited one of us to come back the next summer and work for him for free (usually students come and pay him a fee). I went the next summer, and that's where I learned about cement. I came back to Canyon, where I got an idea for building a place of my own.

"In working on my place, I saved money by using large stuff for which there's not much market—telephone poles, railroad ties, old lumber from a wrecking yard for flooring. If you're willing to build with large materials—using new types of construction—you have to work a lot harder and use different methods and tools. But you don't have to have a pile of money or be subsidized by a bank. That's my objection to the building codes. They want you to use conventional materials so they can check the plans out in advance. I didn't know what I was going to do here when I started, so I didn't apply for a permit. So I had the house a long way before the inspectors saw it. It gave them a chance to learn about hyperbolic paraboloids."

He invites you to share his dinner, which he starts cooking on a wood stove in a corner of the large, unpartitioned space, where he washes, eats, lives. Then he leads the way downstairs to the foundations of the earlier house upon which his is built. In a kind of basement with a low ceiling and concrete-based walls is a faded mattress and blankets, a toilet, a wall-less outdoor shower, a knotted rope instead of stairs. Here, too, the side of the house facing west is left open; a screen of tree trunks and low brush is before your face, with the hill dropping off quickly behind, and another hill of evergreens rising in the distance. The deeper you go inside his house, the more you seem to move outdoors.

"I used eucalyptus here because it's not popular. The eucalyptus poles grow like bamboo. I go in and thin them out; it's good for the trees. I figure I've got something going that will give the redwoods and Douglas fir a break. The prices at lumberyards are outrageous. There are tremendous amounts of wood lying around, and people in building have a moral obligation to use what's available before destroying trees.

"With an Alaskan Sawmill attachment you can make lumber

from logs and fallen trees with a chain saw. It lets you mill any size lumber on the spot, from twelve-by-twelve beams to one-inch. All you need is gasoline and a car battery for blade sharpening. You can stack and age the lumber right on the spot, which eliminates road building—the most destructive part of logging. You can leave the wood natural if you like, keep the sapwood and bark on certain kinds. And you can tie in with tree surgeons to use what they cut."

His dinner is one simple, elegant dish of rice, vegetables, and meat served in a tin pie plate. With it you have tea made from local sassafras root, which tastes like warm root beer. His cups, glasses, and jugs have the amorphous look of local pottery—they were fired in a kiln that used to be next door.

As you sit on his rough-carpentry benches or stools, friends begin to drop by, Canyon neighbors, a tall, friendly young man with a British accent, who stays and talks awhile, and a part-Negro girl with a sullen, quiet beauty, who says nothing for a long time, just stands and watches. She is wearing a tight pink sweater and shades and smoking a cigarette and is sending messages, which he does not seem to be in the mood to receive. Finally she asks him when he is going down the hill, because she is going down the hill and needs a ride. He tells her flatly that he is not, and after waiting a few silent minutes, she leaves; there will be someone else with a car, more pliant. Yet even as she undulates up his wooden steps to the road, you know that she will be back. He represents a pole of the community, Canyon's ultimate political, life, and architectural style, who influences people by example rather than by persuasion. At some time or other, everyone's directional needle seems to swing his way.

"I joined the IWW because I didn't want an ordinary union. I wanted a union I could dig. The IWW still puts out a paper, and they have offices in Chicago and San Francisco.

"I was in jail for four months, in Santa Rita, on a traffic charge. It was a good education. That's where I got to like living without walls. While I was there, the crew of the *Everyman* was brought in, that pacifist ship that went to North Vietnam. Burton Stone was one of the men on it, a carpenter who had gotten into Zen. When he and I got out of jail, there was fifty dollars in each of our property from the Wobbly defense fund. Somebody had sent in our names, and there was a gift, with no obligation. Burton was really impressed by that. He joined the IWW afterwards and eventually became a Wobbly organizer.

"The Wobblies represent organization without coercion or institutionalization. I feel that's what's unique about Canyon; people have built a road and have a Community Club, but there's no coercion. I'd hate to see this place become rigid and exploited. Some people wouldn't object to seeing a city out here, but I would. People look for some big solution—they have contact with city people who come out here and think they're out in the wilderness and don't need manners or concern for other people. It usually comes down to you taking it upon yourself to correct something that's wrong instead of passing the buck to the authorities. The pressure to do that is greater all the time. I hate to see that. I'd hate to see the day that anyone goes down to the grove with a badge on—no matter how psychedelic it is."

Fourteen / Embracing
the Bogeyman

For some of the older residents, life in Canyon had become a crescendo of insults and affronts. The endless flow of odd-looking people, the noise, the nudity, the crazy architecture, the movies, the happenings, the antiwar activities and drug arrests, the newspaper exposé articles, the rudeness, the litter, and the old junk cars were to them, in sum, evidence that these new people were destroying those very things that had attracted individuals to Canyon in the first place. The young people, well intentioned though some of them might be, just did not understand this, because, after all, this modern Canyon was the only Canyon they had known. Since the community itself had changed, something other than the simple love of nature and a desire for independence must be continuing to bring them here, a lust for license, an adolescent flight from responsibility, revealed in their disinterest in maintaining a neat personal appearance and in the primitive ways they chose to live. In their revulsion toward destructive impulses the older residents found themselves drawing closer to those voices outside the community that were now loud in condemning it. There was a time when people in Canyon had told their children, half-jokingly, that the man in the green-and-white East Bay MUD patrol truck was the bogeyman and that they should run from him whenever they saw him coming.

"The kids would be down at the stream, and they'd have to hide," says a man who lived in Canyon then. "The adults might be wandering off in one of the fields or wherever, behind the fences. You'd have to go through a bullshit session with the guy if he'd catch you."

Now that same bogeyman, whose interest, after all, was the preservation of land, trees, and wildlife, began to seem more and more like a sympathetic friend, less bent on destroying natural Canyon than were the people who were moving in.

Seeing themselves isolated, alarmed at their helplessness in the face of fundamental change, a few of the older people, urged on by their children, who had grown up in Canyon but now lived elsewhere, concluded that they must act in concordance with their former enemies or see Canyon become nothing more than a garbage heap of hippie crash pads.

In December of 1968 three long-time residents of Canyon appeared at a regular meeting of the Contra Costa County Board of Supervisors at the County Offices Building in Martinez, where they testified that because of the new, unsavory element now rampant in their community, they were afraid to go outdoors at night. They presented a petition, signed by more of the older Canyon residents, requesting the Supervisors to drive these new people out by enforcing the building codes against Canyon's illegal houses, even though this would mean using purely regulatory ordinances for police purposes and siding with East Bay MUD in its desire to move people off Canyon land. The bogeyman—turned back at the Canyon Store, outbid by the Water Brothers, outwitted twice more in land purchases by individuals—had now been embraced.

In response to this request, a series of inspections was begun in mid-January of 1969 by officers of the County Building Department and the Housing Authority. Without warrants, these inspectors entered upon private lands, took photographs of the dwellings that had been built without permits, and made notes of individual violations at each house. These included not only instances of structures and materials that didn't conform to the building code, but the lack of sewerage facilities, which the county expressly forbade. If a house lacked a flush toilet, the owner could be cited for violating the county building code, and if it *had* a flush toilet, the owner could be arrested for violating the county health code. No matter what you built, even on your own property, there was no way for you to be within the law.

The people living in the threatened houses, watching the inspectors walk about their property and critically examine their work, or hearing about it from neighbors or observing the trampings and scrapings of the inspectors' passing, considered that the older residents, by going to the county, had betrayed them, had violated their fragile privacy, and had abandoned the community's unwritten rule of forbearance.

"Almost every one of the older people had built some part of his house not according to the code," says the President of the Water Brothers; "added a room, put in an illegal septic tank. Yet they say to us, No, you bad people, you built without a permit."

Early in February, 1969, the man from Canyon Construction, accompanied by one of the members of the Canyon Store Trust and the attorney for the Water Brothers, went to Martinez to ask the Housing Authority officers about the results of the building inspections. They were told that in six days all houses built in Canyon without permits would be posted and the occupants given forty-eight hours to leave.

Alarmed at what seemed to them a harsh and unfair use of the inspectors' enormous discretionary powers, several Canyon residents went back to the County Offices Building to speak to the County Housing Co-ordinator. Surely he was aware that there were agricultural areas of the county where people were living in shacks and even abandoned railroad boxcars. Yet these residences, if that is what they can be called, were apparently under no threat of condemnation, although the adequate houses in Canyon were. The housing man said that he would be glad to co-operate with the builders in Canyon in obtaining permits, but that he was being pressured by the President of the Board of Supervisors. He suggested that the Canyon people return the following day and present their case before the Board.

When a delegation of ten Canyon residents returned for the Board's regular session, they were told that they would not be permitted to speak because they were not listed on the agenda. Exasperated at what they were beginning to regard as an official run-around, the Canyon people were directed to the man in charge of the Building Department, who said that he would de-lay the postings until the following Tuesday, when a formal ap-peal could be made, but that the people would first have to discuss the matter with the President of the Board. Finally, after the Supervisors' regular meeting had ended, the Canyon people spoke briefly with the Board President. He intimated that he would not press for posting the houses until the appeal had been made and that he would come out to Canyon and investigate the situation for himself on the coming Saturday. Momentarily relieved, the Canyon residents then returned to their houses.

The following day, February 17, 1969, the county moved into Canyon in force, with inspectors, armed escort, narcotics agents, and the man from the pound with the tranquilizer-shooting gun. The residents, warned in advance, had invited the press and television newsmen to come to Canyon and observe what was happening, and the inspectors and deputies walked along the paths to the popping of flash bulbs and the whir of televi-sion news cameras, posting the illegal houses, and ending forever the illusion of Canyon's isolation. It was the first time in the history of the county that an armed force had been used in a Building Department posting.

———

With the posting of the houses, resurgent Canyon at last came face to face with the interests of the civilization it had fled. Behind every charge leveled at the new houses built in Canyon was a claim in the name of society at large, while every dome, lean-to, and compost pile in the community was a declaration of an actual or fancied individual right.

"My home was declared unsafe because of the foundation," complains one man whose dirt-floor cabin was posted. "The foundation's the earth. The Building Department ruled the earth is unsafe."

By building without first obtaining building permits, the young people of Canyon had been aware that they risked losing everything. Yet, judging from the examples around them—the radically remodeled older houses, which the county had not bothered posting, the rebuilt store and post office, which, as an accomplished fact, the county had approved—the conclusion seemed obvious: if you contended long enough with the opposition—the county, East Bay MUD, the older residents—they would eventually give in. The route to qualification under the law led through defiance of it.

"We realized that if we left the houses, it would be recognizing the evictions," says the President of the Canyon Water Brothers. "If we had been as naïve as they hoped we would be, people would have moved out. But we stayed. We got an injunction. We made an administrative appeal to the Board of Supervisors that we felt this was illegal. It meant that they had to work on the appeal before they commenced with the abatement procedure. This gave us at least ninety days."

Now, by the class-action nature of the postings, the survival of those individual houses was bound up with the survival of Canyon as a community, and the differences among the Canyon young, Water Brothers and non-Water Brothers, owners of old houses, tenants, and squatters were resolved. The county had defined them as enemies and had united them in opposition to itself.

"I'm sure they think we're picking on them," says T. M. Gerow, the county's Chief of Environmental Health. "But it isn't something that faces the Canyon people alone. In this county we have a moratorium in certain areas where if you own a lot, you can't build on it. To the people who have the lot, we're bastards. Our point is that if they wanted to keep this a remote area, in all its purity, they would have to pay the cost."

If the county was intent on enforcing the ordinances against them, the people of Canyon would raise the money to make it go to court. If the county came out physically with bulldozers, it would be physically resisted by bodies. If it insisted that Canyon install an expensive sewer system and become part of a suburban sewer district, then Canyon would install a cheaper, more efficient, ecologically sound sewer system of its own.

Fifteen / The Pony-Express Man's Son

The roomy, unvarnished wooden house rises steeply above a narrow footpath in a series of architectural transitions: redwood steps and braces, an upper deck looking newer than the lower, a wing whose wood is still a pale blond. Inside, the main room is large but fully occupied by the accumulated odds and ends of a life's work: sculpture, portraits, books, a menorah, drawings, an easel, the sophisticated poverty and orderly clutter of a working artist. An iron wood-burning stove heats the living room, which is also a studio, with light bursting through a large fiberglass skylight; it is also a dining room, with a rough-finished picnic table extending the length of the skylight. He himself is such a youthful-looking man, in the manner of the young people in the community, with a full red-brown beard and long hair, lean and fit, his young daughter playing in the corner of the room, and a son named Eagle practicing on a distant trumpet, and an attractive wife, who comes in from the kitchen bringing a cup of tea, that it is a shock to hear him talk about coming out to Canyon in the twenties. Surely he means *his* twenties. Then he mentions that his father was a pony-express man riding between Sacramento and several of the Gold Rush towns, towns that later became ghost towns.

"I've lived in Canyon for twenty-three years and in the Bay Area, one place or another, for about forty. In the early twenties, I had come out here to visit as a child, and I was all over the place. It was called Redwood Canyon then. I've seen a great many changes since. People come and go. Many houses that were here just disappeared, like mushrooms. The water company was always handy with the cash. I've never been able to figure out why it's so hard for people to buy property here, to get bank loans and fire insurance.

"I had a studio in Oakland, and I lived there for about two years in an old stable. It was originally a carriage house for a fine old building. They were tearing out all that property for a freeway, and I had to find another place. I had a model who posed for me at the California College of Arts and Crafts in Oakland, where I taught painting, figure drawing, anatomy, and painter's craft. She brought me out here—she had a little place out here —and told me I could stay until I found something. I wandered around and found two or three houses that were vacated. That's unheard of now. The irony is that all these houses were torn down, and now people are willing to build and live in anything. Anyway, I found this house and had it paid for in a short time. I won several awards for painting and sculpture, which allowed me to pay for the place in eighteen months. It was clean and orderly when I found it, but it needed a lot of work. The original structure was built here before the turn of the century, in the 1880's or mid-1890's. It has been built onto. Changed hands a few times, but there were only two owners. The people I purchased it from lived here from early in the century up until the thirties. To me, here in the wilderness, it was a mansion. I'd wanted to live in a place like this all my life; I'd never found room enough to live and work at the same time.

"When I first came here, I'd reflect that some of the houses were empty, and I wondered why. It was so close to the city. Many of the women were grumbling. Then I realized that they

were interlopers who had come out during the war because of
the housing shortage, that they disliked the discomforts and
wanted only to move out of here as early as they could. The
young people then weren't interested in Canyon. Now they are.
There's a new spirit among many of the young people, a spirit
like the old frontiersmen had, to get away, to get out into the
country and stake a claim—and it is a good thing. Most of them
have practically nothing, but it doesn't bother them. Their
clothes are patched, but they are clean. They're not like the
young people you see in the city. These kids are clean and have a
good, healthy viewpoint toward life. They're very American."

He leads the way downstairs, through rooms he has spent
most of the last five or six years remodeling; the house itself now
seems to absorb most of his time and energy.

"I used to attend the Community Club, but I always felt an
outsider there, probably stems from my work. I was concerned,
certainly not indifferent. But I feel the best thing I can do for
Canyon is to put this house in shape. Anything I've accomplished has been entirely my own effort.

"I used to wander around the hills here and camp out, starting in the twenties. Every summer I headed for the Sierras and
usually spent a month up there. I'd hitch a ride up with a pack
on my back—hitchhiking was simple then.

"Nowadays it's getting to the point where you have to be a
plutocrat in order to enjoy the country. Certain sections of the
public tend to spoil the wilderness for those who would really
cherish it.

"I never noticed any kind of life-and-death struggle going on
in Canyon before this one. There was always the knowledge that
East Bay MUD was willing to pay anyone who approached
them, but in my estimation what they paid was never enough.
The water company bought and demolished three houses right
near mine. Actually it gave me more room and more privacy. I
never considered leaving Canyon when my neighbors left. Oh,
my friends thought I should move to some place like Mendo-

cino, but I asked them how could I live there? Where could I find a house like this?

"Canyon could be turned into a very special kind of residential community, one I don't want to be a part of. I don't want to see a lot of roads put through here and trees cut down. The water company would negotiate and sell to developers—just wait things out. I don't think they're worried about time.

"The young people here aren't going to give up; I know that. Even if hell freezes over. Some of these people would rather die in order to prove that this country is still American and that it's not going to take dictation from organizations that have no interest in the land itself."

Part Two

One / The Man
and the System

Somehow, through a combination of luck, tradition, social circumstances, and the values inherent in the community itself, Canyon had always been able to produce the individuals essential to its survival at the time they were needed. There was Jim, the pacifist and Vigil organizer, who had suggested and led the formation of the Canyon Store Trust; the young tenant of Mrs. Holmes who had founded the Water Brothers in order to acquire her property; the man from Canyon Construction who redesigned the store, then led the large work party that rebuilt it. In each critical situation one man had assumed a disproportionate burden of the responsibility for the survival of the whole community, receiving nothing in return but the respect and gratitude of his neighbors, which, in a community without formal civil honors, political offices, or keys or medals or plaques, became the only local form of power or reputation.

Now, following the postings, the people of Canyon faced a problem unlike anything they had experienced before in its complete antipathy to the community's basic philosophy. In order to preserve Canyon in its rustic state and satisfy the county authorities, it would be necessary to introduce a complete sewage-disposal system, along with the assessments and taxes necessary to install and maintain it, a system tying each house to its neighbor and to the whole community in precisely that kind of permanent civic structure that Canyon had always managed to do without. Faced with this paradox, the community once again produced an individual with the personal convictions and the professional training needed to resolve it. This time it was a maverick civil engineer who preferred rustic surroundings to orderliness and comfort.

A slouching, bush-bearded, soft-spoken man in his late thirties, Doug McMillan had come to Canyon in response to one of the Water Brothers' ads in *The Berkeley Barb*.

"I had been in Korea on a UN project for a company that had a contract with the American government. It was a river basin in South Korea. The project was to reclaim a tidelands area for paddy lands, using sea dikes. The feasibility report took three months. It was like building something on a state line, between two provinces. There was a political hassle, and they were unable to do anything. We were back in Berkeley when my wife saw this ad. It said, 'New Community Forming,' and we came out just for the ride."

Though he knew no one in the community, McMillan had gone to high school in Contra Costa County, and Canyon had been part of the local high-school scene, one of the places where you could go to drink or park and make out. Hoping to become a farmer, he had enrolled in the School of Agriculture at the University of California at Davis, where he discovered that for an individual to begin to farm commercially required initial capitalization of about a quarter of a million dollars. An engineering department was opening at Davis, and he transferred into it, eventually taking his Ph.D. at Berkeley. A specialist in water resources, he now worked for the University, for private companies, and for the government on projects like the Korean tidelands reclamation and as a consultant on the distribution of Colorado River waters in Arizona.

In Canyon, at the hyperbolic paraboloid house at the top of the road, the man from the Water Brothers talked to McMillan about the association, how it worked and what the problems were that its members faced. He explained that a county ordiance had recently been passed prohibiting the installation of a septic tank within 1,000 feet of a stream tributary to a reservoir and that, in effect, the ordinance made it prohibitive for anyone in Canyon to build a house, so that even when you had your Water Brothers site picked out and paid for, there was no assurance that you could legally live on it.

Seeing the community, savoring its close abundance of trees and land without the rules and regulations of a National Forest or Park, talking to people who were actually living there, had brought out the farmer in the engineer. Here was a community of people whose interests were his, living within reasonable distance of the city, in surroundings where you might still hope to build your own house on your own land, plant flowers and vegetables, even raise a few chickens or goats. It took the McMillans about two weeks to decide to join the Water Brothers. In two weeks more they had raised the money.

It was nearly a year before McMillan was able to move into the upper floor of one of Mrs. Holmes's old summer houses, just above the railway roadbed in Canyon. ("The understanding was that people who were living in the houses that the Water Brothers owned would have a year to find something else. The people living here—a crash-pad kind of scene—were eventually evicted.") By then he had become involved in planning that would indirectly set the course for the whole community's future.

"I had been gathering background material on disposal systems for over a year. The previous fall I had presented our own report for a Water Brothers system to the Local Agency Forma-

tion Commission. In our talks with the Chairman of the Commission, he kept coming back to a Community Services Disposal
System, a complete district for tax purposes that, like the school
district, would cover all the private lands in Canyon.

"He led us to believe we didn't need much—a rough estimate, a budget, and a petition. A week after we had submitted a
formal petition for a Community Sewage Disposal System, with
the signatures of ten per cent of the community, the county
posted the houses. It was an indication they weren't about to
play very fair."

Spurred on by the furor surrounding the postings, McMillan
now enlarged and deepened his report. Though his special field
was water resources, not sewage disposal, he was able to rely on
professional sources, existing documentary material, and inter-
pretations by colleagues. He also included some of the letters
between people in Canyon and various county officials, some of
which he considered to represent classics of officialese.

Completed in one month, the "Preliminary Engineering Report on the Canyon Special Services District" proposes a permanent operating system of community public services unique
in this country and perhaps in the world. In a complete de-
parture from traditional utilities planning, where massive ar-
teries are installed to feed a theoretically limitless growth, the
services are instead scaled to the needs of a community gradually
restored to ecological balance, with the utilities district itself
serving, in effect, as a conservation and population-control
agency.

The most remarkable feature of this system is its integrated
philosophic base. Everything about the district—sewage disposal, water supply, financing, operation—is contained within
the larger structure of the community itself, so that the district
constitutes neither a government nor the business interest of
outside investors. It truly inhabits the community it serves.

At each Canyon homesite, sewage would be initially treated
by a cheap, portable Cromaglas air-filtration unit, a modern

adaptation of the traditional septic tank. The waste water, up to 97 per cent treated, would then flow through pipes to a pumping station at the bottom of the canyon. From there it would be pumped up to the top of the hill, filtered through a series of percolation beds until potable, and stored in a 250,000-gallon community reservoir, where it would provide a permanent water supply for irrigation and fire fighting, which Canyon has previously never had. Because no water leaves the community, the balance in the local water table is maintained, and there is no need to pipe in outside water and pay for the installation of yet another service system—a system operated by East Bay MUD. And, because there is no need for the huge mains and pumps necessary to transport sewage to some distant treatment plant, the cost per house for the community sewage-disposal, water, and fire-fighting system is less than two-thirds that of the lowest estimate for a conventional sewer system alone.

Most significantly, because the water is treated at the site, then recycled and restored to use within Canyon, there is no removal and subsequent dumping of diluted or partially treated sewage into any lake, stream, bay, river, or other public body of water, and therefore no increase in the pollution count anywhere.

McMillan's original report leaves several important questions concerning the district unanswered. Financing is one. There is no factual statement in the report of the individual home-owners' ability to pay for the installation of a system whose cost would be as much as one-fourth the assessed value of their houses. How and by whom the system would be serviced and maintained was not made clear. Most serious in the eyes of the county officials who would be asked to approve the formation of the district was the system's originality, its lack of an established, working precedent. In studying the report, they would realize that they were being asked to approve an experimental system on watershed lands.

Nevertheless, the report is lucid, comprehensive in its scope, and prepared with great thoroughness. No fewer than seven alternate waste-disposal and fire-fighting systems are analyzed and compared as to their applicability to Canyon. There are detailed diagrams of the proposed system's filter beds, reservoir, and pump stations, as well as a master plan prepared by an architect, a Canyon resident formerly on the Berkeley Planning Commission. There are professional analyses of Canyon's geology, ground-water patterns, and seismic hazard, a brief history of the community, a thorough breakdown of estimated costs, and copies of related correspondence with county officials, bringing the report, in all, to an impressive 106 pages.

What McMillan had succeeded in designing was a technological organ, a mechanical heart for a dying community, that the body of Canyon might find compatible and accept. What remained to be determined was whether or not the county would permit the radical surgery necessary to install it, whether what was proposed as a cure for one of its member communities might not endanger the health of all.

Long before the first eviction notices were posted, the county housing, building, and health authorities were aware that the residents of Canyon were trying to create a special district of their own for sewerage, water, and fire protection. The county had even scheduled hearings on the district. Now there were delays, postponements, and rumored meetings between county officials and representatives of East Bay MUD. The commissioner who had first recommended formation of a Special Services District now announced that he was opposed to it, and officials of the county's Central Sanitary Sewage District, who the previous year had said they would accept a special system in Canyon, now reversed themselves and insisted that the only acceptable system was a conventional gravity sewer, which would cost an estimated half-million dollars—more than four times the total assessed value of the land and houses.

On April 15, 1969, the houses that had been posted for illegal building were posted again, this time for abatement as a public nuisance. The application of the county building code was so literal that the housing officer making the recommendations was later to admit, under an attorney's cross-examination, that had the code described the lack of a Picasso painting as rendering a house hazardous to life and health, he would, in this situation, have cited it as such.

Amazingly, in this proscriptive climate, the Local Agency Formation Commission, swayed perhaps by the thoroughness of McMillan's report, or by the enthusiastic endorsement of it by people like the Moraga Fire Chief, approved the formation of the Canyon Special Services District, on condition that it also be approved by the County Board of Supervisors. On this acceptance, at least for further study, the community's legal counsel was able to delay abatement, pending the outcome of the Supervisors' hearings, which would probably continue through the summer.

While the hearings would at least lend the community a few more breaths, it was a loan secured at great risk. The entire question of Canyon's survival—the formation of a utilities district, the legality of the new houses, the question of demolition —now rested in the hands of five men who sat at a political intersection, where the interests of the county collided like the automobiles of stubborn, willful drivers.

In Canyon, the question of a services district crystallized the attitudes of old residents and new.

"The issue was joined over the district," says the President of the Community Club. "But it could have been anything. If the young were in favor of selling to the water company, the old would have been against it."

Now, with each circulated petition, each canvassing call for support, each appeal for money, every property owner found himself with the opportunity and burden of declaring himself for or against the young people who had taken over the community. Anyone with a grudge against them now had an outlet for it and a cause in which to enlist his neighbors, while those who barely knew the young people were asked to side with them against friends they'd known for years. Regular estimates were made of individual support, straw polls in which everyone knew or speculated how everyone else in Canyon felt. Eventually, the vote broke down to a majority—mostly young and long-haired —in favor of the district, and a minority—clean-shaven and conventionally dressed—opposed, with a group of long-time residents undecided and therefore subject to considerable pulling and hauling in between.

But before the Supervisors' hearings could even begin, the community was faced with a new crisis, this time its most violent and literally inflammatory to date.

Two / Holocaust

At this time, the only pipeline connecting Canyon with any outside place was one that people generally didn't even know about. Carrying neither sewage nor water, it had been installed as recently as 1965 by the Shell Oil Company and was used to pump gasoline from Shell's refinery in Martinez to storage tanks in Oakland and San Jose. Though the ten-inch pipe extended the twenty-five-mile width of Contra Costa County, it was buried everywhere but in Canyon, where, out of indifference or opportunistic cost cutting, the pipeline as it crossed San Leandro Creek had been left exposed despite the objections of the Moraga Fire Chief, who was responsible for the area. It was assumed, once the pipline was installed, that everybody would forget it was there, which was pretty much what had happened. Life in Canyon continued in its rustic, unmechanized way, while the fuel for thousands of cars, trucks, buses, and airplanes flowed unnoticed over the creek and under the redwoods to the urban centers of the south and west.

Then, early in 1969, Shell's entire Western Regional Division became engaged in a bitter labor dispute that extended into a strike and ultimately a consumer boycott of Shell products. The strike dragged on for two and a half months, until March 17, when the Shell workers consented to return to their jobs, though there had been no agreement and no new contract. It was in this atmosphere of labor-management grudges and soured consumer relations that, on the night of March 17, someone dynamited the Shell pipeline at its most vulnerable point.

At the time of the blast, Shell refinery workers had just completed pumping a large quantity of automobile fuel to San Jose, and though the line was shut down, there was still gasoline inside the pipe. As soon as evidence of a leak appeared on the refinery pressure gauges, a Shell pipeline superintendent was sent out to locate the break.

Meanwhile, in Canyon, thousands of gallons of Shell gasoline were gushing out of the broken pipe into San Leandro Creek, where the current carried the fuel and its thick fumes downstream, past the newly renovated store and post office and in the direction of the Canyon School. People in the community, startled by the concussive thump of the dynamite blast, hurried down the hillside to the area around the store to see what had happened and to talk to their neighbors, only to find themselves nauseated by the thick and clinging odor of gasoline. The fumes, heavier than air, would not rise, but lingered instead near the windless floor of the canyon, creating a serious fire hazard. No one seemed to know what had happened or where the gas was coming from. Frightened, the residents nearest the store called the Moraga Fire Department and the Contra Costa Sheriff's office.

By the time the firemen and deputies arrived, people were fainting and vomiting from the fumes, and car engines were stalling for lack of oxygen. Some women and children were being evacuated to the parking lot of the Moraga Safeway, while sheriff's deputies urged everyone to remain calm, assuring them that there was nothing to worry about.

When the Shell pipeline man, dispatched by the refinery, located the break and saw the size of the rupture and the amount of raw gasoline that was trapped within the narrow creek bed, he hurried up to the store and told the people standing there to run for their lives. Eyes streaming, gasping for breath, the people scrambled up the hillside, accompanied by the deputies, who abandoned their cars, as the Shell man stepped into the phone booth next to the store to call the refinery. One of the fire-department engines, able to start, was driven up the road from the store to where the road was wide enough for the truck to be turned around.

Suddenly, in a series of thunderous roars, the whole night was lit with leaping sheets of orange and yellow flame. Far up on the hillside the windows of the houses appeared to turn red, and one woman saw an orange flicker on her ceiling so vivid she thought her bedroom itself was on fire.

With tremendous heat and force a wall of flame swept down the creek, consuming everything in its path, tree limbs, patrol cars, trucks, small animals, garbage, brush, debris. A film of fire clung to the surface of the creek and glowed along the edges of the store. Compressed inside the patrol cars, the gasoline fumes exploded with such force that the live ammunition inside began sputtering off, the doors were blown open, and the roofs bulged out in huge, grotesque bubbles. A motorcycle and the telephone booth beside the store were melted by the heat, and water left by recent rains in a concrete retaining wall "popped" in such a way that the wall was left as pock-marked as if it had been raked by machine-gun fire.

The Shell man, who had been inside the telephone booth when it exploded, staggered around outside the burning store in agony, mortally injured. All his clothing had been torn off, and even the hair had been burned from his body. Firemen and Canyon people rushed to help the man, who was coherent and even helped his rescuers move him onto a stretcher improvised with blankets. More than ninety per cent of his body was covered with burns, and he died two days later in a San Francisco hospital.

"From the top of the hill, the fire looked like a huge orange ball," says a young Canyon man. "I thought they'd dropped the bomb at last. I went running down. God, it was hot. It was actually a kind of relief to find it was only a fire."

As news of the fire storm spread, additional fire-fighting men and equipment were rushed from departments in Oakland and Contra Costa County. Bizarre rumors, fed by fear and panic at the sounds of a blast, exploding ammunition, and police- and fire-department sirens in the night, swept through the communities nearest Canyon. A mad bomber was loose. The hippies had risen in armed revolt. A drug dealer's secret laboratory had exploded. Everyone in Canyon was dead. Both highway approaches to Canyon were, in truth, blocked by sheriff's deputies who, in at least one instance, informed returning residents that they were too late, that the whole community was devastated.

Within Canyon the atmosphere of violence and terror produced a confusion of its own. One young man, standing beside the open door of a truck about six feet from the creek, was knocked into the truck and across the seat by the blast, which burned his hands, face, and buttocks. As he lay on the seat, a trail of flame came up under the truck. The young man, fleeing in panic, staggered out and plunged through the barbed-wire fence across the road, away from the community, and into the watershed lands of East Bay MUD. Scorched and frightened, he clawed and scrambled up toward the top of the ridge opposite Canyon, stumbling along unmarked deer trails in the dark, streaked up an incline that takes a hiker a half day to climb in daylight in a matter of two hours. Reaching the fire trail, all scorched face and hands and torn clothing, he followed it to the nearest house, a ranger's cottage. The ranger's wife, home alone, listening to accounts of the bombing and fire on the radio, opened her door to a tattered, hairy figure and panicked, concluded that he was the Hippie Bomber, and slammed the door. The rejected man took off doggedly down the fire trail to the next house, also a ranger's home, where he received a more hospitable welcome. The young man's wife found him in a hospital in Moraga the next day, after having spent the whole night searching for him.

Meanwhile, along the creek above the school, the redwoods were smoking eerily in the dark as fire hoses and searchlights were played upon them. Thirty pieces of equipment and nearly seventy men were crowded into the narrow road, trying to contain the flames. The highway to Moraga blared with sirens and flashing lights, and in Canyon and around the Moraga Safeway lost people milled about in search of family and neighbors.

Had it not been for a heavy rain only the day before, the whole hillside and all the homes on it undoubtedly would have been consumed in the kind of fire storm that, in recent years, has devastated suburban canyons near Los Angeles. But showers and then a low-lying mist had so dampened the ground, trees, and cover that, after an hour and a half, the fire was contained only twenty feet from the bridge to the Canyon School. The store and post office were gone, however, and the trees continued to smolder until after daylight.

In the morning the sleepless residents of Canyon wandered through the rectangle of twisted metal and charred beams that had been the Canyon Store. A powder of fine, gray ash lay over everything like a dirty snowfall. Some people sifted through the ruins for salvageable items, while others simply stared, dazed, at the wreckage of their work. The ruined store and bare, blackened trees gave the whole community a desolate, gutted look. Seven men had been injured, one fatally burned, six less critically hurt by flames and smoke. Eleven cars had been destroyed, the banks of the creek scorched, the redwoods defoliated as if by napalm. Gradually, as the young people surveyed their losses individually and as a community, their shock turned to rage at the company that had installed the pipeline in such an unprotected manner and at the authorities who had permitted it. When, about midmorning, a Shell work crew appeared to repair the pipe, they found themselves face to face with a group of angry Canyon residents, sitting on the torn and ruptured metal, vowing not to move unless the pipeline was placed underground. The men from Shell, who might have entertained some theories about the young, long-haired people's role in the blast, appeared sobered by the reality of the damage and the threat that the fire had posed to the entire community. No man would set a blast like that so close to his own house. Anyway, it was imperative that the pipeline be restored to service, and with television and the papers out covering the fire, a sit-in by the residents would make an ugly scene. The Shell workers expressed regret for the blast, the injuries, and the damage, and, as the Canyon people understood it, said the company would repay the people of the community for their store and post office and reimburse the man who had been living over the store for his belongings lost in the fire. Shell workers and Canyon people shook hands on that as the Canyon residents removed themselves from the torn and jagged pipline. Soon the line was in service, pumping Shell gasoline once again through Canyon, this time underground.

No one has ever been charged with setting off the Shell pipeline blast, a charge that, with the death of the pipeline superintendent, would also include murder. It has been rumored to be either an act of union gangsterism or of revoluntionary politics, but the search for evidence has apparently yielded nothing more substantial than the six-inch piece of C-4 plastic explosive found by firemen shortly before the fire started. A full-page ad run by Shell in San Francisco Bay Area newspapers, offering a $50,000 reward for convicting information, has produced none.

The area near the Canyon Store looks now much as it did the morning after the blast and fire. The redwoods, bare and blackened for half a mile up the creek, their few remaining upper branches a parched brown, have begun to bud with green again, and it appears that they will respond to the Shell fire storm as they have to previous calamities, as indignities to be endured and outgrown. Around the store itself the loose debris and the few standing charcoal timbers have been removed, but the remaining concrete foundation has a blackened, bombed-out, forgotten look that is twice an eyesore, because it misrepresents the attitude of the whole community. Architect's plans have been made to rebuild the Canyon Store and with it a new Canyon Post Office, replacing the red-white-and-blue trailer that serves as a temporary post office now. The architect's drawings are finished, Canyon Construction is willing to organize the work crews, and the people of the community are ready to donate their time and labor once again to the reconstruction of the store, with or without the required permits. The problem this time is that the money to rebuild the store was promised, but the promise has not been kept.

Officials of Shell Oil maintain, despite what the Canyon people understood from the repair crew, that the company is not liable for any of the damage done by the blast. The people of Canyon, if they wish to collect on their claim, must go to court, which in a civil case in Northern California means a delay of about two years and the financing of a full-scale legal prosecution. All to collect a sum that would probably not equal the cost of the reward ad, let alone the reward itself.

Through all this the people of Canyon, like the redwoods, persevere. There is so much to contend with that there is little time to brood. And with so much against their community, each day of simple survival is an important victory. No one, at least, is alone. And even from devastation and death lessons can be learned.

"It taught us," Doug McMillan says of the Shell blast and its disheartening aftermath, "the value of a handshake."

Three / The Unconsumer

He climbs in big, springy strides up the steep path to his man-made knoll, carrying four refilled plastic distilled-water jugs. Offered a hand, he divides the load and leads the way on up the hillside, where the path seems to lose itself wandering among the maze of trees. He is a gentle, intense man, lean, big-eyed, with thick brown hair and a wide mustache, and as he climbs, he explains over his shoulder that he believes in using water the same day that he draws it, that it loses "life" if it sits in storage. Abruptly, he plunges off the path, through some brush, tightropes along a nearly vertical stretch of hillside to where an arc of small plants is screened by trees and shrubs. Opening a jug, he balances on the hillside, one leg bent, the other stretching, and begins pouring water on the plants.

"In case you're wondering, these plants are marijuana."

Asked whose land it is, he smiles. "The water company's."

Going back down the hill, he explains: he grows his crop only for himself, although at one time he was in drug dealing, which he came to despise.

"I mean, when they just point the gun at you and say, 'Give

me the money,' you know it's time to get into something else."

His house is a one-room cabin made almost entirely of old window glass. Glass in the shape of shutters, leaded windows, sections of skylight. Above the cabin is a long, narrow tree house in the crotch of a large oak. The tree house is also largely made of glass and commands what must be a five-mile panoramic view of evergreen forest, stretching beyond both ends of the canyon. The cupboard is outdoors, and almost at eye level with the trees that top the ridge on the opposite side. Pots, pans, plates, knives, and spoons are exposed to the air on a plank resting on two logs. On ledges and blocks in the yard outside are a hairbrush, soap, toothbrush, and shaving equipment. A mirror is nailed to a tree. There is about everything a Marine drill sergeant's sense of individual discipline and the importance of taking care of things.

Inside the house, the thick trunk of the oak tree forms part of one wall, and shoes are left on the dirt floor, next to its roots. There are sleeping bags on the floor. There is a simple table, phonograph, speaker and tuner, a battered telescope, and a wood-burning stove.

"Before I came here, I worked in the photography darkroom of the Astronomy Department of the University of California in Berkeley. I was senior photographer in the department, and for five years I worked in a darkroom six floors up in a building standing on cement. After a time my hands began to tremble, so that I had to use one hand to steady the other. I knew that there was a center of myself somewhere that was truly me, and that I had got off my center, and that if I could cut away everything that was fucked up, I could have the kind of integrity a person should have. So I gave up my job and told my ex-wife I couldn't go on doing what I had been doing to pay alimony and child support. For a while I took out my frustrations in speed—racing away to places as fast as I could on my motorcycle. All over the state. Mexico. Then I began to study Indian music, and something started coming through me that was beautiful. I lived on what I'd saved and what I could pick up working part time. I wanted to study music and enjoy nature.

"I walked around Canyon a lot of times. I had lived out here for two years once in somebody else's shack. I did a lot of work on it, but it wasn't right. So I moved back to Berkeley. But I had been touched. So I built a house here. It was nothing more than a wide spot in a steep path when I started. The retaining wall was made simply by clearing the forest of debris. I use my own garbage and shit as fill and cover it with dirt. The glass I use I got from glass-replacement houses. They take windows out of old houses and put in new ones. I asked one of the glass-replacement men what they do with the old glass and found that they just throw it away. He said I could just come in and haul it out, and I did. I got as many as sixty panes of glass in a single load."

As he talks, it grows dark outside, the trees across the canyon and the houses on the hillside below slipping into gloom, leaving only sounds behind: voices, sitar music, a dog's bark. A girl, blonde, wearing one of the gownlike print dresses common to young Canyon, has materilized out of the dusk and is preparing dinner on the wood stove as he bathes with cold spring water in the dark outside. She lights a Coleman lantern and starts mixing a Canyon-style meat-vegetables-and-rice meal. The girl says she went two years to Bennington and two years to the University of Wisconsin, came to California, where somebody told her about Canyon, and now isn't sure what she wants to do.

Does she live here, too? There are two sleeping bags. But, though two people can sleep in a one-room cabin, they can't really live there, can't read, work, entertain, withdraw. Instead, the young people without legal status, the tenants and squatters, tend to visit among the other small owner-built shacks and houses, dropping in first on this hillside dweller, then another, returning to one house to eat and sleep. Social electrons, they orbit the larger, legal houses that are the nucleus of Young Canyon. "Home" is actually the common hillside, the pathways through the trees from unfenced lot to unfenced lot, seeing whom you want, when you want, in whatever state you unexpectedly come upon anybody.

"My son's built his own tree house up the hill from here," the man has said proudly. "He's seen the way I live. He's seen me making love here, and that's a beautiful thing."

Naked, dripping from his bath, the man steps back into his house, dries himself with a towel, puts on a robe, sits on the floor in a lotus position, and shivers slightly for a good ten minutes.

"At first I couldn't walk up the hill without stopping. I had forgotten how to walk on the earth. Now I'm strong—I mean, I'm not big, but my muscle tone is back, and I can walk up and feel good about it.

"Like a lot of other people in Canyon, I'm deep into Indian music. I play it by myself, and sometimes we play it together. Sometimes we play the sun up.

"I wanted to see how far I could go on nothing. I've eaten squirrel and even snake. I was going down Pinehurst Road on my motorcycle one day when I saw a king snake, and I hit him. The meat didn't taste very good, but I think I cooked it wrong. I made the skin into a belt and put it on my hat."

As mysteriously as she came, the girl has gone, melting into the dimensionless black outside. Finishing his one-dish dinner, he goes outside, washes his plate and fork, and comes back in with a large supermarket case, a dozen browning bananas rolling about the bottom.

"I pay no rent. No utilities. I need almost no money. I get leftover food from Safeway. They discard huge quantities of usable produce. As for the winter, I simply get used to being cold. Now conventional heating makes me uncomfortable when I'm around it. Out here, living this way, all your feelings come back. There's a lack of the guilt you find outside. I got back on my center. Like, I went up to Canada, and I was at home on the earth there."

He lights up an after-dinner joint, resumes the lotus, and tells how he has become intimately aware of wildlife.

"Like the doves. Pigeons you might call them—a city word. They come into the trees and then all face the sun at dusk. I used to wonder why, and then I thought if a hawk was going to attack, that's the way he would come, from out of the sun. Once, after a hundred-mile-an-hour gale on the coast, there were hundreds of doves here, come for refuge."

There is a fluttering hoot of a cry—an owllike sound—which, he explains, is his son coming up the path. He opens one of his windows, and cupping his hands and blowing into them, he makes the ancient Indian-and-small-boy noise in reply, and continues improvising riffs of his own. Soon the whole hillside erupts as one, two, half a dozen cries from other houses like this on the hillside echo back and forth across Canyon. For five or ten minutes it continues—a theme and variations transforming the hillside into a forest full of owls or solitary primitives communicating in a language of their own.

His son is about fourteen, long-haired, shy in the presence of a stranger, and settles on one of the sleeping bags to eat a banana.

"For a while I taught biology at a prep school up on the coast. Man, it was crazy. Stone buildings. Go out and cut your own wood. The students were very unhappy. My own kids even stopped eating. So I left.

"This house was one of the ones that was posted. The inspectors spent two days walking around the community, and they didn't get all the illegal places, just some. It was like having rats in the community. They stapled the notice to my door and didn't come in. When I saw the notice, I was insulted. I tore it off.

"I guess the reason that this community works is that we live more in nature than people do in the city. This is a natural community, and the community comes together in the face of threats from outside. There's a feeling here that what a man does is his own business, unless he is hurting the community.

"I felt all along I had a center, a pinpoint—and I tried to get on it. The center was outside of me, and now it isn't. I'm here, standing on the earth. That tree *watches* me."

Four / A Sewer
to the Moon

The house of John Muir, a National Historical Site of staggering uncongeniality, sits on a rise in the Alhambra Valley just inside the limits of the town of Martinez. A huge, dun-colored, ugly Victorian mansion landscaped with palms and other exotic trees, the house was actually built by Muir's father-in-law, a well-to-do landowner and fruit-grower, who willed his mansion and his lands to his son-in-law in the hope of making a gentleman farmer out of him. Muir, a gaunt, weather-beaten, abstemious man, a self-taught naturalist who somehow managed to combine the job of operating a successful fruit ranch with a career of campaigning for the establishment of what became the American system of national parks and forests, preferred sleeping outdoors under almost all circumstances and once diverted a stream to run through a Yosemite cabin so that he might observe it continuously. On at least one recorded occasion, Muir picnicked amid the ruined redwoods where the community of Canyon now stands. One can imagine the reaction of a man who was to spend his lifetime writing, lobbying, wheedling, making speeches, and testifying in court in behalf of the preservation of America's forests to the sight of what was then a sea of redwood stumps.

The town where Muir is enshrined is an old Gold Rush port on San Pablo Bay, set among the low, dry hills of northern Contra Costa County. It is a town of stunted growth, modest old houses, and a brick-building business district, where it sometimes seems as if the date on the daily newspaper must be 1915. Aside from a pair of oil refineries on its outskirts, Martinez's major enterprise is now the county; and the Contra Costa County Offices Building, which looks like the kind of oblong plastic box a giant expansion watchband might come in, is by far the tallest structure in town. Here, on an afternoon in August, 1969, when the Savings and Loan's rotating temperature sign is registering over ninety, the citizens of Canyon have come to present the case for a sewer system of their own before the Board of Supervisors.

In the Supervisors' Chamber, a large, windowless, air-conditioned room, with indirect lighting, complementary green tones, and one ornamental wood-paneled wall, the representatives of East Bay MUD, the Central Sanitation Department, the County Health Department, and the Public Works Department stand in a cluster before the bar, waiting for the Supervisors to arrive, discussing the Canyon issue among themselves with a mixture of nervousness and condescension.

"He can't be objective about the thing," says a man with just a fringe of white hair, earnestly holding McMillan's report. "It's just too close to a major source of water."

"The worst thing about it is this volunteer business," says a man carrying a clipboard and with a row of pens and pencils clipped in the pocket of his short-sleeved shirt. "Volunteer projects are tremendous—I belong to the Lions Club. But you can't operate a sewer system with volunteers."

As the county men stand talking in a group to one side of the center aisle, the delegation from Canyon files into the chamber, the Canyon people taking seats in the front rows of the bank of chairs on the opposite side. While the Canyon spokesmen have made halfhearted or unsuccessful attempts to appear in coats and neckties, there is a preponderance of Army shirts, Levis, sandals, headbands, long hair, and beards, giving the group the disorganized, vaguely threatening look of a segment of crowd at a rock concert, or of hitchhikers along a contemporary American highway—of people who can assault you without physically touching you.

Between the two groups, Canyon and the authorities, there are exchanged glances but no conversation, as both sides confer among themselves and busily leaf through papers. Among the Canyon people, heads down, smiling nervously, there is a self-consciousness at being off home grounds, combined with a traditional distrust of institutions, now manifest in the sight of the officials all standing together in opposition to them.

Following the first delegation from Canyon comes a second, a group of older residents, who take seats on the same side of the aisle as the Canyon young but behind and apart from them.

A woman in a print dress, her face rigid with disdain, walks up the center aisle and takes a seat among the older residents.

"Is that Mrs. Marks?" a bushy-haired, mustached young man from Canyon is asked in a whisper.

He looks at her, then whispers back. "I don't know. All straight people look alike to me."

There are, in all, about forty people from Canyon, almost evenly divided between old and young, and perhaps twenty county and East Bay MUD officials across the aisle, all waiting as the President of the Board opens the afternoon session and the Supervisors dispose of preliminary matters.

Seated at the center of a raised dais, below the county's seal, the President of the Board, as Supervisor representing the county district including Canyon, cannot be without private feelings about the community. For years, every complaint about Canyon, every indignant letter or phone call or rumor about noise and drugs and runaways received by the Board, has crossed his desk. His neighbors and friends—suburban homeowners to whom Canyon represents the iniquities of city life they moved here to escape—are concerned for their children and property, and it is their demands for action that are the loudest. To maintain an unbiased view in such circumstances, to approach the proposed district as something more than a hastily improvised scheme whose real purpose is to still criticism, would require a sanguineness of temperament perhaps unreasonable to expect in a professional political man. Nevertheless, as he introduces the matter of the Canyon district and the homeowners' petition in its favor, it is with the old politician's unprejudicial air of chronic fatigue, as though he has heard everything a thousand times.

To the young people from Canyon the hearing represents a unifying experience, a forum for the presentation and defense of an attitude toward life, a chance to confront all the powers ranged against them and publicly demand justice. There are, after all, five Supervisors on the Board, not all of whom are considered hostile, and the votes of only three are needed for approval. Moreover, the district has been approved by the Local Agency Formation Commission, and the Supervisors have never been known to turn down a LAFCO-approved measure. It is in a spirit of affirmation, then, that Canyon's young element has prepared its presentation, beginning with a smooth, temperate speech by the President of the Canyon Community Club, reviewing the differences between community and county, followed by the introduction of an architect's master plan for Canyon, complete with mounted sketches and tissue overlays.

While Canyon's resident architect stands beside a large sketch of the hillside, Doug McMillan slouches at the rostrum before the Board, describing the physical organization of the proposed utilities system.

As McMillan speaks, the Supervisors seem reluctant to look directly at him. Uneasily, they find themselves reduced to a student-teacher relationship by the presentation of a technically detailed idea. The man is obviously informed on a subject about which they are ignorant. Yet they are the approving authority here. Questions must be asked, but they can no more challenge the man on his own terms than could the average high-school physics student challenge his lab instructor. No, the thing to do is to keep the questions at the layman's level, at the risk of appearing naïve, or of being rudely turned aside.

"What if one of the pumps goes out of whack?" a Supervisor interrupts. Then, says McMillan, the other pumps take over.

"How many systems such as this are in operation?" asks another. McMillan doesn't know of any.

"You intend to store and use—what's the term?—secondary treated effluent. Is this done anywhere?"

Yes, says McMillan. San Francisco uses secondary effluent. Stow Lake in Golden Gate Park is secondary treated effluent.

The Supervisors look at one another. Stow Lake is San Francisco's most popular recreational boating area, an urban pastoral preserve of picnickers, rowboats, abundant greenery, and ducks. For three-quarters of a century, those picnickers, boating couples, and ducks have been communing with reclaimed sewer water.

In the official silence, McMillan resumes. Canyon has an abundance of springs and wells and makes good use of its existing ground water, so that it is vitally important that the community maintain its water table. It is a simple equation that if you export sewage, you must import water. But the Central Sanitation estimate does not include an additional $2,500 per house that would be required to bring in an outside water supply. The Canyon estimate is based on a maximum of 80 houses, with an average of five people per house. Such a system would help control Canyon's population density, preserve the wooded nature of the community, and maintain its ecological balance. The minimum sewer line, on the other hand, can serve 600 houses, and 600 houses would drastically alter the character of the community, laying waste most of Canyon's natural vegetation and turning it into a conventional suburban development. For these reasons, and others that people in favor of the district will present, he urges approval of the Canyon Special Services District.

There is a reluctant silence when McMillan has finished his presentation, as if he has already answered questions that the Board members haven't thought of yet. Finally, the President of the Board is moved to comment. Very good, he says. Quite a thorough report.

Now other spokesmen from Canyon—the President of the School Board, the President of the Water Brothers, the attorney representing the residents—fill out the portrait of their district. It becomes, in their description, a kind of commonwealth, where each house is independent of all the rest, yet each is dependent on the district—broad, inclusive, humanly responsive, ecologically sound; an inexpensively installed system, requiring frequent care and maintenance, in a community where the practice of constructing, then caring for things—the school, the road, the store, the water system—is ingrained.

"We don't want to become part of suburbia against our will," pleads the President of the Community Club. "And we're not interested in East Bay MUD's plans for the future—we've suffered enough from that in the past."

For one brief, tantalizing moment, it seems as if the presentation has been so thorough, so persuasive, that even the opposition must be satisfied, must agree to let the residents of Canyon build a sewer system of their own. Then the representatives of the county and East Bay MUD begin their rebuttal. Using the same data, referring to the identical wooded hillside, they depict another Canyon district, inadequately financed, poorly engineered, and a threat to the public water supply.

East Bay MUD is diametrically opposed to the creation of such a district, says the utilities district's Assistant General Manager, a feisty, Trumanesque man, reading a prepared statement. "The Canyon district is neither in the public interest nor economically feasible."

Capital costs, budget, and maintenance are grossly underestimated, the system is not practical from an engineering standpoint, and it permits the discharge of sewage underground on a watershed. Besides, any argument that Canyon can't afford a conventional sewer is utterly specious.

"To anyone familiar with recent events in Canyon, it is readily apparent that the Water Brothers and other newcomers to Canyon have no lack or shortage of funds."

As he leaves the rostrum, he is angrily hissed from the Canyon side of the chamber.

"Why, I could hardly get my own people to operate such a system," says a man from the State Department of Public Health. "Even the most highly skilled operators often can't keep a waste-water system operating, and even if they could, such water would be unsuitable for fire fighting and irrigation."

"The system is too dependent upon individual units," says an official from the Department of Public Works. "And I question whether the Cromaglas dealer can assure operation and replacement in the event of mechanical failure."

"The proposal is not definitive," says a county health official; "it keeps changing."

The line of officials filing to the rostrum seems endless. As they testify, the case against the district seems to grow in weight, if not in fact. While on the Canyon side of the chamber, people are squirming with rage.

"They're presenting an extreme description of what can happen," whispers Doug McMillan. "They're bullshitting."

"I must dispute the conclusion of my brother engineer," says the Manager of Water Distribution for East Bay MUD. "The proposed system is complicated, sophisticated, and mechanically dependent, fraught with problems for even a highly trained operator." As a man responsible for the water supply of over a million people, he says he must have some guarantee of such a system's safety in watershed lands.

"What you need in this situation," says the Water Distribution Manager from East Bay MUD, on his toes with earnestness at the rostrum, "is a sewer system that's sure-fire, like Apollo Eleven. You need a system that will get you to the moon and back."

Leaving Martinez, whether you are going southwest to San Francisco or directly south toward Moraga and Canyon, you pass the large, square house where John Muir spent his last days, a house that now overlooks two freeways, one of which is named for Muir.

The Supervisors' hearings had been continued for two weeks, following the introduction of letters opposing the Canyon district from the Regional Water Quality Control Board, the County Director of Planning, and the County Administrator, as well as personal objections by various individuals. Among these was the curious testimony of a Moraga doctor who claimed, in an excruciating stammer, that he had seen things in Canyon that offended every one of his moral and religious sensibilities.

"I'm well to do," said the doctor, "but I've lived among poor people. To turn this thing over to these people is like turning your dinner table over to people who go out and eat slop like the hogs."

He testified that once, about two years before, he had wanted to live in Canyon and that he still visited there. He was a man who had made it a weekend practice to distribute bottled water along Pinehurst Road so that passers-by would refrain from drinking from the creek, which, he told the Supervisors, "could carry hepatitis, typhus, syphilis, gonorrhea, and plague." Such are the passions aroused by the habitation of man in natural surroundings.

In John Muir the thought had inspired a passion of a different order, though every bit as intense.

Canyon

"Tell me what you will of the benefactions of city civilisation," Muir once wrote, "of the sweet security of streets—as part of the natural upgrowth of man—If the death exhalations that brood the broad towns in which we so fondly compact ourselves were made visible, we should fee as from a plague."

Five / "If I'm Wrong,
Then People May Die"

The offices of East Bay MUD's Water Distribution Department are in one large warehouselike room, broken into cubicles by wooden partitions that don't reach the acoustical-tile ceiling. Over the cubicles, and from desks in an open area in the center of the room, leak the voices of shirt-sleeved men, fragments of cryptic telephone conversations with mobile units, distribution checkpoints, repair crews, and customers. The merging, busy voices, combined with the lack of windows and harsh fluorescent light, give the department an air of isolated immediacy, like a combat battalion headquarters or a newspaper city room, the sort of grim surroundings that make it easy to believe in the chaotic state of the world outside.

In his large corner cubicle, surrounded by books and file cabinets and a framed photograph of his family, the Water Department's Managing Engineer welcomes the chance to express his objections to Canyon, both professional and personal. Youthful but not young, wavy-haired and bow-tied but not that old, he speaks with the near-zealous earnestness of a man whose job has taken on certain moral and social justifications, and he tends to state his opinions in eschatological terms. He is a man of vague literary ambitions (there is mention of a book linking Old Testament prophecy with contemporary Egypt), who is given to astonishing conversational gaucheries. ("We caught them with their pants down," he says of the Canyon people's plans for a sewer system, without a trace of humor.)

He is the man ultimately responsible for the quality of all water supplied by the water company, and has been pressing for the acquisition of lands in Canyon to eliminate a pollution risk for fifteen or twenty years. "I'm legally responsible," he says. "So you bet I go back and pick through the bushes and the rocks. The buck stops at this desk."

He has indeed walked the hillside, examined the creek and the springs, attended the meetings, argued over construction sites, and made enemies. He says that he has had to have his telephone number changed because of threatening phone calls, that high-school kids in the area have let the air out of his car tires, and that he has even received insulting Christmas cards, including one from Canyon that enclosed a leaf and a note that said, "I'd have sent poison oak, but it's out of season."

His distrust of Canyon's young people and their district is something more than the professional's disdain for the enthusiast. Deep, sinister forces are at work in Canyon, he hints. He claims that some of the older residents are so frightened of their neighbors that they are afraid to complain of abuses directly to the police, and that, in fear of retaliation, they call East Bay MUD instead and ask the utilities district to complain. He says that Canyon residents have thrown rocks and pointed guns at his men, and that he will no longer send men to Canyon alone. He believes the people in Canyon have a short-wave radio network that they use to alert one another when inspectors arrive, and that using this, they can pick up and move some of their illegal domes and other small structures at the authorities' approach. The Canyon people are likable, he concedes, but ruth-

less in their determination to live as they wish, even if it means
going outside the law and jeopardizing the health of others.

"In August and September of 1969, we took the report on the
Canyon district and analyzed it. We are in the business of building and operating water services. We have years of experience,
and we very carefully reviewed McMillan's report and made par-
allel estimates. McMillan was talking theory and concept, and
in theory and concept it would have worked. But in theory and
concept almost anything will work.

"What they were proposing would have been the most
sophisticated sewage system in the State of California from the
viewpoint of difficulty of operation—and they proposed to operate and maintain it with volunteers. The whole proposal was full
of should-would-mights.

"We caught them with their pants down. We are specialists
in filtration—not them. The design and maintenance of their
filter system was bad. Who would rehabilitate their sand-filter
system? We have men working twenty-four hours a day on ours,
and we have a dandy time trying to keep it operating. They
wanted to leave theirs unattended. What control would there
be on testing? Would they run samples every day?

"The Cromaglas units aren't in use in other than an experimental situation in California. We had our engineers call the
Cromaglas people back in Pennsylvania, and they had only
seven to ten units on test. We were unable to find anyplace in
the United States or elsewhere where Cromaglas units exist as
an accepted means of sewage disposal.*

"I don't think they have the right to jeopardize the public

---

* According to Milburn J. Hynes, Executive Vice-President of the Cromaglas Corporation, Williamsport, Pennsylvania, more than 2,000 Cromaglas air-filtration units have been installed throughout the world; and
tests from Switzerland, Sweden, Canada, Pennsylvania, Delaware, and
Virginia, and testimony from homeowners and health officials "indicate
that Cromaglas Wastewater Treatment is a superior device."

water system just because they are frontier types. They've had poor sanitation for years out there, from what I've seen, a Shigella epidemic, garbage. Who says they can maintain the most sophisticated system in California? They have no operating experience, only a tremendous drive to exist. They take the position that if you just let it get in, it will work. Well, who is most impotant—a few people who are so desirous of living in a pristine environment that they will do anything to stay there or 100,000 people depending on that water supply? Who wants to take the chance? I don't. A lot of people are relying on my judgment. If I'm wrong, then people may die. In Riverside 18,000 people got sick from contamination directly attributable to the water supply. In Madera a hole dug by a gopher produced contamination of a reservoir. In storms you can get runoff organisms at a filter plant within two to three hours. We have such a great amount to lose that we can't afford to be wrong. And all we have is the law, facts, and scientific procedure.

"By their own testimony before the Board, they were proposing to tinker with an experimental system on our watershed. It's an experiment that shouldn't be tried in that place. If the line is broken in Canyon, then private landholders can march all over our watershed."

Six/Aim High,
Feel Low

Among the young people of
Canyon, there remained a feeling that their district must eventually be approved, a confidence born partly of their own desperate will to survive, but also of the belief that the people who
knew what was best for the Canyon land were those who lived
most intimately with it. Drinking water from the wells and
springs, wearing paths into the hillsides, carrying in wood and
food and carrying out garbage and sometimes waste, they
bought large joys in installments of small discomforts, and felt
themselves in harmony with an order beyond that of Contra
Costa County.

"The moon isn't full until it comes up just as the sun sets,"
says the President of the Water Brothers. "I didn't know that
until I lived in Canyon. I'm learning to tell time and the time of
year by the stars. Weather patterns are apparent, and the
growth of plants is obvious."

Perhaps life in Canyon seemed sweeter, rarer, now that it was
threatened with extinction. It *had* become more harmonious.
The conflicts among the younger people seemed to be less frequent and more easily resolved now that there were actual

enemies outside. Internal bickering seemed merely a waste of political energy. A group of young people, some Water Brothers, some not, began spending most of each Saturday going to the San Francisco Farmers' Market, buying wholesale lots of vegetables, fruit, and cheese, and trucking them back to Canyon, where, using a groceryman's scale, they apportioned the week's food in the schoolyard. Others, hoping to rally support for the district, went from house to house among the older residents, where occasionally doors were slammed in their faces, trying to talk to people and handing out mimeographed information explaining McMillan's plan and assuring those on fixed incomes that the tax burden would not exceed twenty-five dollars a year. As a minimal security measure, a man living near the bottom of the road had begun stopping people who seemed to be wandering about aimlessly and asking them whom they wanted to see and whether they needed directions.

One night, not long before the last of the Supervisors' hearings on the district, the interested residents, almost entirely young, gathered for a monthly Community Club meeting in a classroom in the Canyon School, squeezing into the children's desks, sitting on the low tables, ringing the room: a spectrum of youth, in every wave length from short-haired 4-H country kids born and raised in Canyon to bearded heads in psychedelic-patched coveralls. There was a bulky-sweatered grad student type who looked as if he had just hopped out of a sports car, a bedraggled, pregnant teenybopper, and an old man with a white beard, who looked like Gabby Hayes. The meeting contained them all. No one was denied his say or seemed to be afraid to speak. There was no ganging up on anybody. The President of the Community Club, intelligent and unofficious, chairing the meeting in a sweat shirt while toddlers staggered around the room babbling and large dogs heaved in sleep on the floor, imposed no order stronger than *Robert's Rules*.

"Something ought to be done about people walking around the community with guns and shooting things," a man with a nervous, abrasive manner, wearing wrap-around sunglasses, began. "Like, I have this thing about guns. I went through this scene in Berkeley with a sniper. A man and a girl with me were shot through the head. Killed. And I was shot through the arm. And now the sound of a gun, man, it blows my mind."

This released a flood of local gun-horror stories, tales of stray bullets puncturing walls, of suburban kids with 22's roaming the community hunting "wild dogs." People started proposing laws and penalties. The community should be posted against hunting. No shooting, a $500 fine, with the section of the state penal code quoted on the sign.

Then a 4-H Club-looking youth who had been sitting on the floor, the son of old residents, rose angrily to his feet.

"I've lived and hunted in Canyon for twenty years, and I'm going to keep hunting no matter what any sign says."

"Well, that's okay," said the man who wanted to ban guns, "because you're Gordy and you know where to shoot and you're not going to shoot where anybody's living and that's groovy. But what about people coming in from outside?"

"Gordy has a point," a pudgy man, with wild Rasputin-looking black hair and beard, commented. "If we put signs all over against all shooting because most people don't like it, then the next thing, there are signs against motorcycles because some people don't like them. Before long, it's like the city, with signs against everything because people are afraid to go up and talk to one another."

Expressing, dissenting, discussing, deciding, the people of Canyon were carrying on, in a positive sense, the activities of freedom. It was, in fact, government by town hall, with all the people—or as many of the people as cared to attend—in one room, with no distinctions between administrators and governed, and each citizen a participant. In Canyon, government by township, Emerson's "unit of the Republic," abides and endures.

It took half an hour of hard argument to hammer out an

agreement, with a principle encountered at every turn. There would be two signs posted forbidding shooting, one at each entrance to Canyon, directed at outsiders, fashioned by local craftsmen in a suitably rustic design.

A few minutes later the President of the School Board, heavy-set, smoking a pipe, suggested for the twentieth or maybe the two-hundredth time that Canyon residents, when they see people lighting fires, tell them to put the fires out.

"Kids from Orinda and Moraga have been coming out and building fires in the grove. The Moraga firemen have to come and put them out. They don't like to come, and once they're here they usually start looking around for somebody to cite."

The only representative of the old Canyon present at the meeting, he had been dealing with the physical concerns of his community for nearly twenty-five years. Neither complaining nor resigned, he seems to have accepted this obligation as part of his daily life, like shaving.

"What about those NO FIRES signs we posted in the grove last year?" a young longhair asked.

"Which ones are those?" said the Club President.

"They were wooden and carved and kind of antique-looking."

"Somebody burned them."

For weeks, campaigning within Canyon had been at ward-election pitch, with door-to-door canvassing, pleas for funds, straw polls, and formal requests for exclusion from the district making everyone in the community intensely aware of his neighbors' politics. Now, on the day after Labor Day, 1969, the people of Canyon sat in the spectators' seats of the Supervisors' Chamber, the old Canyon in one bloc, the new Canyon in another, with the faces of the Board jutting above the raised dais and the representatives of the county agencies sitting watchfully at official tables off to one side, listening to the last heated opinions and final cold facts, hungering for answers, yet fearful of conclusions.

The additional testimony in the hearings had only reinforced each side's position. Canyon's attorney had presented letters of intent from twenty people, pledging $50,000 to finance the original construction of Canyon's system; the county's Chief of Environmental Health testified that, in his opinion, they wouldn't be able to maintain and operate it. A revised estimate of the installation cost of a conventional sewer proved to be substantially unchanged from the earlier half-million-dollar figure. The only financially realistic, officially acceptable alternative to a Special Services District for Canyon seemed to be the same: no Canyon.

"Everybody talks about environment," says Ted Gerow, the county's Chief of Environmental Health. "Save this, save that. If this is the case, then the Canyon area would be best off as a park. But the people in Canyon don't want public enjoyment of the area. They want personal enjoyment. This is a metropolitan area. You can't say one little part of it is entitled to preservation unless you make it a public park."

To which people in Canyon reply that a civilization that offers men only cities, suburbs, and parks is a failure.

"When I was growing up," says the President of the Community Club, "the world was *done*. The parks were made, the benches were built, the springs were capped. Everything was in place. You didn't ask questions. It was enormously frustrating. We don't want that to happen here."

"People read the books," says Doug McMillan, "they acknowledge the imminent disaster, yet they refuse to take the steps necessary, preferring to stick to the familiar death-oriented course. They are still within the Machine. The Machine works very well, but it is working toward a climax species. It produces machine people, and eventual disaster."

At last the speaker's rostrum is empty, and an anticipatory hush falls upon the spectators and the members of the Board. The questions have all been asked and answered. Now it is time for interpretation and an intuitive response.

147

Supervisor Thomas J. Coll, once a St. Mary's College football lineman now a large, jowly lawyer resembling a big-city policeman, breaks the silence. Supervisor Coll says that he doesn't believe in septic tanks but that he has been encouraged by the testimony of the people representing Canyon.

"These people are doomed unless a system such as this is approved by the Board. Nobody else has come up with an economically feasible system."

He cites a letter from Joel Fort, formerly San Francisco's Deputy Director of Public Health, endorsing the Canyon district as "a necessary social experiment." Coll moves that the proposed Special Services District for Canyon be approved.

There is another long silence while the other members of the Board look down at the dais or out over the crowd. The representatives of the county agencies are looking at the young people from Canyon. And the people from Canyon begin looking at one another. There are shakes of shaggy heads, rueful glances; some people stare at the Supervisors as though willing them to speak. But not a hand or voice is raised in support of the motion. There is no second.

One of the Supervisors is moved to comment. As a Supervisor, he says, he would be taking a chance in going along with this motion ("Take it!" a Canyon supporter shouts), and because it does mean taking a chance, he says he will not do it.

A second Supervisor explains his silence. He says that the testimony on the Cromaglas system is just opinion, that the system is not proven and should only be approved if it is applicable to the whole county.

If the system works in Canyon, Coll suggests, it could be used in places in his district where people live beyond existing sewer lines. The first Supervisor disagrees. "What would happen if we approved this today and next Wednesday other people from other areas come in and request it?"

Now the President of the Board resumes his presiding role in the hearing, formally denying Coll's motion for lack of a second.

He says he has withheld his opinion on the motion until now, but that he agrees with the Supervisors in opposition.

"We must rely on our Health Department, State Public Health Department, and Pollution Control Officers, who have gone on record in opposition to the Canyon district."

He moves that permission to form the Canyon Special Services District be denied, and this time the vote is four to one in favor. The district is rejected, and the hearing is declared over.

Among the people from Canyon, the concluding statements go almost unheard in the atmosphere of bitterness and resentment. After all the months of delays and appeals, after all the canvassing and fund raising and planning and politicking, they are legally where they were the day the houses in Canyon were posted. They have been brought face to face with the sad truth that the surest consequence of ambition is dejection, that in aiming high, a man condemns himself to feeling low.

In the corridor outside the chamber, they linger in an orgy of anger and injury, clustering around Doug Page, their attorney, with questions. What will happen now? Will we be evicted? No, he thinks attrition is more likely. The county feels time is on their side.

"What am I supposed to do?" one young man asks urgently. "Should I invest more time and money in building my house with no septic tank and no permit?"

"You know the answer to that," Page says. "No."

One man explodes into obscenities against all the officials in the room.

"It's just their job." A friend attempts to soothe him.

"Sure, it's their job. But it's *my house!*"

Off to one side of the corridor, Doug McMillan walks out quietly with his wife, pale, shaken, looking now more like a bearded old man than a bearded young man.

"I thought we had it won," he says, stunned, uncomprehending.

Someone asks him for a copy of the report, and McMillan

hands him one as though throwing away hundreds of hours of his own work.

"This won't be of use to anyone now."

In the crowd around the lawyer, someone suggests that they set up a working demonstration of a Cromaglas unit in Canyon. A permit is required for that, he is reminded. It is loosely agreed that there will be a meeting to plan strategy.

The plans for the district, the community, and individual homes have all been aborted; there remains one absolute value: apocalypse.

"It's time to quit spending our money on lawyers," says a bushy-haired young man, "and start putting it into bullets."

He is the same man who, a few nights before, had wanted to ban all guns from Canyon.

Seven / Organizer

Canyon's best-known collective-or-commune (the members themselves are undecided which is the more accurate term) is located in neither a dome nor a shack, or even on the young side of the village. It is instead in a roomy old two-story house, with a broad, comfortable deck set back from the Redwood Highway and bearing a strong family resemblance to the neighboring houses of the older residents. Like those houses, this one is under no threat of condemnation, and it is leased from the man who started the Port Chicago Vigil by an organization called Vocations for Social Change.

Sitting on a bench on the deck, listening to the wind soughing through the eucalyptus leaves overhead, watching the men and women, who all seem to be twenty-three years old and who introduce themselves by first name only, going in and out of the house, talking to the boyish, soft-spoken, sparse-bearded young man who started the organization,* you realize that this is actually an office, and the people here office workers, manning type-

---

* Since this interview, he has left Canyon and returned to Tennessee, where he is a traveling representative for VSC.

writers and printing machines and postage meters, in closer contact with a network of associates outside than with the people who live immediately around them.

"We get about half a dozen visitors here a day," the founder ("initiator," he prefers) says in a half-hillbilly, half-hipster style that combines his Tennessee origins and his experience as a campus social activist. "A lot of them are parasites who look at this and say, 'That's where I want to be.' People don't understand how much work you have to put into things and how serious you have to be. If they like this kind of thing—this is a model—then people should try to do this thing elsewhere. Kids don't understand that you have to weave the fabric of your life yourself."

Vocations for Social Change is a job clearinghouse whose purpose is to match the most socially useful work in America with the people best qualified to do it. Reading the bimonthly bulletin,* you notice that the jobs listed are almost uniformly demanding and low-paid. Yet the bulletin is devoid of preaching, extremely practical, and almost entirely free of romantic or revolutionary escapism. It is aimed at the idealistic young, and its tone is a simple "put up or shut up."

"I used to be a campus traveler for New Left organizations like SDS, and for the American Friends Service Committee. It seemed to me after a while that my best days were not when we planned demonstrations but when we talked to people about what they were going to do after school. I felt there was a need to find ways for people to find full-time—as opposed to part-time—involvement. I felt this especially in the South, where I did most of my work. You could see people getting more enjoyment out of full-time work. Also, the organizations were all understaffed and short of trained, experienced people.

---

* A one-time-only newspaper, *From the Canyon Collective,* was published in 1970 by some of the same individuals, but not under VSC auspices, as a guide to alternative living in response to the invasion of Cambodia.

Organizer

"In the summer of 1967, while I was working in Berea, Kentucky, I put out a pamphlet called 'If You Want to Work Full-Time.' It was helpful, but not helpful enough. We felt that what was really necessary were people who could write up what it means to work as a full-time social activist. At this time I was being funded by friends, and I asked in my letter, 'What do you think about taking on a girl as a full-time worker?' The girl, Ellen, was hired, and we collected these essays, but it didn't do enough. What was needed was concrete stuff, not bullshit rhetoric—a movement-type employment bureau. So we started Vocations for Social Change.

"VSC is a decentralized clearinghouse for persons struggling with one basic question: how can people earn a living in America at this time and ensure that their social impact is going to effect basic humanistic change to our social, political, and economic institutions?

"The bulletin is essentially a directory, a how-to-do-it publication, with job listings (being an organizer for a textile workers' union in the South, teaching and helping with community organizations in Appalachia, counseling GI's), alternative institutions (new communities, co-ops, homes for runaways, social centers in ghetto areas), peace groups, education/research, coordinating the movement for change. The publication comes off fairly heavy. There's no bullshit. It's distributed through key contacts so that it doesn't end up as another magazine in people's garbage cans. It's not a ZAP comic that everybody can pick up and groove on. The main idea is to stimulate rising occupational-expectation levels in society as a whole. People won't put up with shit when they know other people don't have to."

In his commitment to society at large, in his dedication, and in the regular rhythms of his work, he is at odds with the unrestrained spirit of Young Canyon, and he knows it. While sympathetic to organizational efforts like the district, which the VSC supported, he remains apart from the day-to-day life of Young Canyon.

153

"We came to Canyon in January, 1969. It was a very heavy decision. The fact that there would be more work involving the community—the road, the Community Club—presented a certain threat. We were mostly sympathetic to the environment, but we didn't want to be seduced by it.

"I differ from a lot of people in Canyon in that I make value judgments about things. I am an initiator involved in the process of struggle rather than being acted upon, being passive. Waiting for vibrations.

"We live here as well as work here. We have a staff of eight now, and we make most decisions by consensus. We're supported by donations, usually from people who send in an inquiry letter with a buck thrown in. We also have a number of middle-class supporters. We try to have as widespread a knowledge of choices as possible. We're referred jobs from other organizations, who pass them on to us. Also, we exchange subscriptions with underground papers all over the country. The circulation depends on our finances, ten thousand one issue, five thousand another.

"All the jobs we offer are jobs that will support you, at least as far as room and board. When it really comes right down to it, I've found that there are fewer really serious people than there are serious employers. If push comes to shove, and you offer them very large responsibilities and low pay, as opposed to small responsibilities and high pay, most people, when the chips are down, prefer the less-hassled life."

Eight/The View
from Flicker Ridge

Barring nuclear or ecological catastrophe, it is easy to project what the Canyon of the remote future—two or three generations from now—will look like. It will have returned to the redwood forest that it was two centuries ago, an anonymous ravine among the redwoods, where dark, damp pathways wind through tall tunnels of trees. Within the next ten or fifteen years, this part of the county will probably be made a regional park, for the county voters who rejected a park bond issue in 1962 must eventually yield to pressures of their own suburban growth. Though East Bay MUD has sold land earmarked for parks to developers before, the public's attitude toward that kind of thing has fundamentally changed. And so has East Bay MUD's.

"If Canyon is sold to developers, I'll quit my job," District Secretary John Plumb says flatly.

But the long view is an inhuman view. It does not tell us what will become of the people who inhabit Canyon now, of the future of their efforts, their institutions, and their architecture. It reduces them to abstractions.

In the hills above Canyon, a man named Al McCosker ekes

out his living raising cattle, trying to preserve an older, Western way of life. A member of the Canyon School's first graduating class, McCosker has resisted the changes around him—the mounting population pressure, the proposed Canyon district—with a stubbornness that the younger people in Canyon can admire.

"If you own more than ten acres these days," says the man from Canyon Construction, "you get paranoid about vandalism. People want to come and frolic in your hay. So something good about the West is going—that whole idea of hospitality and generosity."

As Al McCosker's Canyon is ultimately doomed, so is Canyon Construction's. Each is a man defined by his land, and cannot be what he is here somewhere else. Time is running out for both, because America has run out of Canyons—rustic enclaves within metropolitan society, where men of small means can live out on the rim, and away from the restraints of urban life. It is no longer possible to live at Walden, and walk to Concord.

"If you want to keep a five-acre estate, you have to pay for it," says Ted Gerow. "If the cost of it gets to be too much, then you just have to dispose of it by sale. It's regrettable, but that's something we just can't control."

"When they can face that reality," says Gordon Laverty, "that you have to pay for a sewer, then they can surmount that reality. We're saying, 'You're not being realistic. That's not how life is lived.' "

What is passing from metropolitan America with Canyon is the frontier-anarchist belief in the liberating power of land, the conviction that what a man does on his own property is his own business, that in working a piece of land, a man improves and transforms himself.

"I prefer to live with as little shelter as possible," says the man in the see-through hyperbolic paraboloid house at the top of the road. "It's miserable at times, but we had no serious illnesses in this house last winter. I miss my privacy, but it isn't worth shutting yourself in."

"I had a ranch house, a lawn, and a crew cut," says Doug McMillan, reminiscing as he engineers the construction of a chicken coop. "It took me six years to get my standard of living low enough so I wouldn't have to do what I didn't want to do for money."

What was once an individual nester or squatter dodging a county sheriff has become a man caught in a net of official agencies whose mesh is too fine for him to slip through. Nowadays, only commercial builders of apartment houses, office buildings, or restaurants can make a practice of risking building first and applying for permits later. It takes a corporation to be a rugged individual.

Probably the people living legally in Canyon now will be able to remain until that future time when their property is acquired for a county park. As long as the septic tanks function, East Bay MUD will not attempt to force the owners of the old Canyon houses off their lands. In April, 1970, a new East Bay MUD General Manager, John Harnett, wrote the President of the Canyon School District that the company had abandoned the land-purchase policy that had governed its actions in Canyon since 1951.

"What this means," wrote Harnett, "is that we will no longer actively attempt to acquire unsewered private lands on our watershed simply because they happen to be there."

Harnett is an engineer, promoted to replace a man who resigned under internal pressure because of his unpopular public policies. According to Bob Kahn, the *Lafayette Sun*'s East Bay MUD-raker, Harnett is a reasonable man who is not interested in maintaining an untenable position. After re-examining East Bay MUD's twenty-year investment in Canyon—more than half a million dollars paid for ninety-five parcels of land, including sixty-nine houses, sheds, and other "improvements," all of which had been demolished, leaving eighty-six acres of vacant lots on which the company paid taxes and from which it drew no revenue—Harnett must have been astonished.

The money spent on land acquisition alone would have been enough to sewer the entire community.

"Let me assure you and the other residents of the community," Harnett concluded in his letter, "that's EBMUD's desire is to live harmoniously with its Canyon neighbors. We do not want to eliminate your community; we do not want to subdivide it; we do not want to harm its unique physical and cultural environment in any way."

Harnett backed his conciliatory words with reparatory deeds. Soon after he had sent his letter, work crews from East Bay MUD began physically rehabilitating the company's face in Canyon. One Monday a gang of men with bulldozers, assisted by Canyon residents, cleared a site for a permanent refuse dump in an unsightly trash area alongside the old railroad bed. The utilities district brought in a number of free garbage cans, and replaced the barbed wire and prosecution-threatening signs along its property with attractive fences of low timber rails. Now, coming upon the community, you no longer felt the abruptness and the sense of official neglect that, in the past, had encouraged the random dumping of trash and the abandonment along Pinehurst Road of stripped and stolen cars. An armistice seemed to have settled over the borders between the company and community, and perhaps the beginnings of a peace.

Yet, had the people in Canyon not repeatedly defied East Bay MUD—and the law—to remain on their land, the community would not have survived the past twenty years. Canyon, as it now exists, is a community bound together by resistance, individuals joined by a constant, common struggle. Now there remained people in Canyon who were continuing to defy the law in the same manner: the Water Brothers, who had built without permits; the squatters, who had built without deeds—almost all the people in the shacks and domes and experimental houses on the hillside. And their future was as uncertain as ever.

With the defeat of the district, the reprieve of these illegal houses had expired. Any dome, shack, lean-to, or tree house built without a permit could be legally abated and torn down as a public nuisance. There was no prospect of any building permits being issued for new construction in Canyon again. And a Canyon where people were not free to build and experiment and reinvent themselves was a Canyon that had begun to die.

"It's an extremely fragile community," says Sim Vander Ryn, Professor of Architecture at the University of California's School of Environmental Design, "an invaluable architectural and social experiment. The houses in Canyon seem to me to be the perfect use of the technology advocated by Buckminster Fuller for the past thirty years.

"All kinds of people from around the country and all over the world are beginning to come to Canyon to study how to build not only a house but a community. I've told our student architects that if you want to learn how to build, go to Canyon.

"The law ought to be helping these people instead of operating against them. No commercial builder is going to follow Canyon's example. No contractor is going to put in the kind of hours these people do—unless he can find carpenters who will work for fifteen cents an hour. People who build for money don't build for love."

On September 29, 1969, the illegal houses in Canyon were posted by the county again, declared a threat to public health and safety, and ordered demolished within forty-five days.

Once again consciences were offended, minds grew determined, and Canyon's guerrilla combativeness began to reassert itself. The posted homeowners met and discussed, with varying degrees of desperation, an appropriate response. Some were for lawyers; others preferred weapons. Ultimately, they settled for both in the person of William M. Bennett, a San Francisco advocate of consumer causes, and bête noire of the public utilities interests of the Far West.

Bennett, a short, feisty, immensely likable man, controversial former Public Utilities Commissioner, with a gift for inspiring among the executives of California's gas, electric, and telephone companies the impotent fury that gas, electric, and telephone companies arouse among their customers, contested the postings in a series of hearings that continued through the winter, spring, and summer of 1970, and included more than 100 hours of testimony.

While the hearings dragged on inside a spare, claustrophobic room in the County Offices Building, outside the year moved through its seasons. Indian summer disappeared; the fog tumbled in off San Pablo Bay; the city of Martinez was drenched with winter rain. Beyond, the culture at large, with increasing velocity, seemed to be moving through climatic changes of its own. The human heart, which Rousseau once described as moving from nature to violence to morality, seemed to be having strange palpitations, murmurs, the warnings of some mass terminal seizure. In December, Charles Manson and his flock of carnivorous sheep were indicted for mass murder in Los Angeles, and the whole idea of new communities began to acquire old, sinister undertones. In the spring, Berkeley's metaphysical rebellion turned violently physical in the rioting, rock throwing, bombings, and bloodshed that reached a climax in the full-scale rebellion and martial counterinsurgency of People's Park. And in San Francisco, a man accused of homicide hitched a ride out to Contra Costa County, where he was arrested while looking for a place called Canyon, where he'd heard anybody could hide out with no questions asked.

Nine / Chaos and Order

P anting and complaining, the news teams from the television stations accelerate down the steep path from the top of the ridge, cameramen gasping beneath their equipment, reporters brushing dust from their suits, tightroping on planks across a series of ditches to a plot of land, where a geodesic dome and a view of evergreen forest form a backdrop for squires and knights of the electronic news, preparing for a joust on an isolated hillside.

Each team shoots establishing footage of the house, the trees, the hillside; then they begin interviewing, reporters with hand mikes nodding attentively as the residents of Canyon and William Bennett and the County Counsel representing the Housing Authority talk about the houses, the community, the clashes with the authorities. Spokesmen and newsmen ride a seesaw of exploitation, the first seeking a forum, the second a beat.

"There is a valid, human reason to make allowances for the homes built by individuals in Canyon," Bennett is saying to a camera, "just as individual allowances are made for older homes under 'grandfather clauses,' which exempt them from subsequent building codes."

Around the dome, opposite Bennett, the County Counsel, wearing a sport shirt and chinos, is telling a reporter that the question is whether the people in Canyon should be exempted from the law. "If they are, then so will be a builder who wants to build a thousand substandard tract houses elsewhere in the county, as one exception engenders other exceptions."

Gradually, the level of antagonism on both sides involved in the abatement hearings had risen. The Canyon people whose houses had been condemned were showing the strain of what was now years of legal proceedings. At least one of the posted houses had been abandoned and its owner had moved away, and two married couples among the Water Brothers had separated. During the hearings, people from Canyon, grown irritable, had begun interrupting testimony and openly disparaging the remarks of the County Counsel, and the hearing officer had started issuing warnings with the grim defensiveness of a Judge Julius Hoffman. What was once a procedure conducted with some levity had soured into ideological debate.

Now, with the testimony on both sides concluded, the principals had moved with relief from the stark hearing room out to Canyon for an on-site inspection of the posted houses, an inspection that Bennett decided deserved the attention of the news media.

The clear air, the sunshine, and the crammed-together ride up the hillside in trucks and jeeps seemed to have mollified hard feelings. As posted homeowners walked and talked along the paths with the County Counsel and the hearing officer, the very mildness of the day seemed to be offering testimony in behalf of settlement, moderation, compromise. Only the building inspector, here to serve as a guide to the posted violations, seemed to have maintained his rigorous frame of mind. Wearing coveralls, carrying camera and note pad, he was now crawling under the foundations of a house, now striking out along a fresh trail, sniffing out additional violations and new construction. When he charged off to examine a brushy hillside where, he hinted, a suspected but unposted house was a-building, the hearing officer declined to follow.

"I don't want to see anything I'm not supposed to see," the officer said firmly, and continued walking toward the next posted house.

For the television reporters and cameramen, the assignment was proving futile, a physically demanding expedition that was producing little or no usable news footage. After the first few houses, the routine of packing a forty-pound camera along a narrow, winding path in hot sunlight and then standing still, holding your breath while shooting footage of what seemed to be just another hippie shack, began to be a distasteful, then loathsome, ordeal.

"I don't know about you," one sweating cameraman said to his reporter partner, "but I'm with the county."

"Next time, *we'll* call *you*, Bennett," a reporter yelled sarcastically.

Before long they had drifted away, disconnecting their equipment and hurrying off in station wagons painted with huge television-channel numerals, to gather other sensations for the collected evening news. An afternoon tide of shade flooded the canyon hillside, and the line of people moving from house to house began to shorten. As they walked up the steep paths, the hearing officer, the County Counsel, and the Canyon longhairs would now and again pause for breath outside one of the small, delicate wooden houses, almost Asian-looking in its minimal intrusion into the wooded slope, sit in a group on a bank of dirt or on a rough bench, or lean against the trunks of trees, and argue in a relaxed, philosophical manner the merits of life here and the dangers it represented to the rest of the county. Away from the echoing official halls, with the cameramen gone and the formal legal language replaced by common speech, the outside world began to seem illusory and only Canyon real. Talking face to face, Canyon men and county men seemed to be establishing a mood of peace and harmony, and to have arrived at an understanding that no man was going to do something knowingly harmful to another.

Suddenly, in a swirl of angry shouts and dust, two men appeared scuffling, with a choked, seething violence that brought the inspection party to its feet.

Faces flushed, grappling, the President of the Canyon Community Club and the Housing Authority's building inspector appeared, fighting, grunting, and swearing with frustration and rage. Quickly the onlookers jumped in and pulled the two panting and glaring men apart. The inspector had been taking pictures, the Canyon man charged; he had told him not to, and he had continued taking pictures anyway, so he'd tried to grab his camera. According to the inspector, he had been deliberately punched. Canyon's man had won the round—the inspector's nose was bloodied—but he had lost the fight. The inspector announced that he was filing charges.

Now the accumulated ill feeling of twenty abatement hearings seeped into the atmosphere on the hillside, and old images of corrupt, arbitrary officials and violent, drug-crazed youth stood like ghosts among the people on the hill. There were murmured apologies, assurances of good will, and handshakes, but no one really believed them. The brief moment of peace and harmony had passed. The woods, familiar minutes before, were a battleground once again, and the people who had seemed so much alike, once more strangers. As the officials returned to their cars and drove out of the community, the inspector holding a handkerchief to his bleeding nose, no one had any doubt which scene from their Canyon tour would remain strongest in memory.

Along the road that winds and climbs through Canyon, the wheelless, engineless hulks of cars have, like exorcised evil spirits, departed. At the level strip near the bottom of the road, where transient teenyboppers once dawdled, glowered, littered, a recycling center—the model for five that will be placed about

Canyon—now reminds the community of its strengths instead of its weaknesses. The slag of rustic life—discarded garbage, cans, plastic bottles, rusted bedsprings, leaking mattresses, abandoned toys—is gone. Given the chance, the people themselves have done what public representatives failed to do: they have brought order to Canyon.

In the months between the conclusion of the abatement hearings and the announcement of the hearing officer's report, a new generation came of political age in Canyon, with new ideas and opinions and a desire to break the circle of county action-Canyon reaction-legal confrontation that had consumed so much community time, money, and energy.

Accepting the change in East Bay MUD's policy toward Canyon as the sign of a sea change among officialdom as a whole, this new leadership undertook its own civic and social repairs, a house cleaning with symbolic overtones, a pruning and weeding of the community's own garden.

With the co-operation of East Bay MUD, the wrecked cars were hauled out of Canyon's pathways and ditches, and garbage cans were restored on water-company lands. The redwood grove beside San Leandro Creek was tidied up and its use restricted to Canyon residents. And the Community Club began regular inspections of septic tanks and privies.

"No one wanted to continue fighting a court case," says the club's new President, Tom Trippe. "We decided to try and make the most reasonable proposals we could."

On June 1, 1971, at the invitation of the Canyon Community Club, Contra Costa County's Establishment itself—the President of the Board of Supervisors, the Director of Environmental Health, the Health Department's Chief Inspector—came to the Canyon School to discuss with representatives of the community the problems between Canyon and the county.

On May 21, the Supervisors had adopted the report of the county hearing officer, who had recommended abatement of ten of the sixteen posted Canyon houses. Now, in the face of further legal appeals, the probability of unfavorable publicity, and the Scroogelike turnabout of East Bay MUD, neither side seemed anxious to resume battle.

"They seemed tired, too," says Trippe of the county officials, "and conciliatory. Everybody seemed to feel that people had better things to do with their time."

With something positive to offer from both sides, the small trades which are the essence of compromise could begin.

On roughly half the posted houses, where people were unable or unwilling to apply for the necessary permits, it was agreed that the residents would move when ordered to do so, but that they would be given occupancy permits and time to resettle.

Two of the posted homeowners were given temporary permits for existing septic tanks pending construction of new houses on the same sites.

Two of the other structures were added as "rooms" to existing houses.

One house was approved pending submission of a property description and a map.

The county officials agreed not to have future mass condemnations in Canyon, but instead, if postings are required, to undertake them on an individual basis.

The county's 1,000-foot limit on septic tanks was amended so that it is no longer retroactive in Canyon. Houses that did not have septic tanks when the law was passed can now apply for them.

With the reconciliation of its differences outside the courts, and the physical transformation of its road and pathways, Canyon now assumed not only a clearly defined legal status, but a new atmosphere, a new "feel," less atomistic, more homogeneous. For the first time, there is an air of permanence to Canyon. But the end of outlawry has brought the confinements of reform. Blunt warnings now are nailed to the trees facing the outside, forbidding trespass, camping, guns, fires. The grove is closed. Canyon is a restricted community.

"We hated to do it," says President Trippe, who lives in one of the posted houses, "but things were getting out of hand. I woke up one morning and there was a complete stranger in my kitchen, trying to fix breakfast."

Canyon is what it is because it is the only way it could endure; although it is restricted, the restrictions are not wealth and race, but energy and taste. What defiant independence preserved, compromise has readmitted to the public realm. A rustic community remains in metropolitan America. An ancestor lives on in our house.

Ten / Bareass in the Pines

I found him in a small clearing below the fire trail, where the knobcone pine trees grow so thick and close that it is almost impossible to see the small geodesic dome until you touch it. I had to call his name—"Doug? Doug?"—until his answers led me to him.

The dome is about the size of one small bedroom, with four cutout pentagonals that serve as doors, windows, and skylight. The over-all effect is a curiously soothing mixture of shelter and exposure, as if the house had evolved around the man who lived in it. There is no furniture inside except for a small table with a few oranges and some other organic-looking foods.

He was sitting outside, cross-legged in the warm sunlight, naked except for a string of beads and sunglasses, his beard and hair long and untrimmed. He offered me an orange, then climbed through one of the door-windows into his house and brought the orange out. Then we sat, overlooking the trees and the hawks circling over the hillside, and talked.

He says that he has become a revolutionary. He believes, out of his own experience, that the existing, technology-oriented system is incapable of the fundamental change necessary for human survival; that "the earth can't support the American way of life."

His voice is calm, almost diffident, as he talks about Canyon's future, his own, mankind's. Only when the conversation turns to the dispute over the district does the tone of his voice and the tension of his body begin to change.

"The people at East Bay MUD are nice, they are polite, they are sincere, and they are trying to bullshit you. The district was not a front. It would have functioned. The budget items described as essential by East Bay MUD are not all required by law, and those that are, if the proposal didn't meet them, it wouldn't have been approved by LAFCO.

"The work would not have been done by volunteers. It was based on an estimate submitted by Canyon Construction, a licensed contractor, paying scale wages—actually better than scale —for all work. Plumbing would have been contracted to a licensed plumber.

"The problem of maintenance is essentially a philosophical question of high installation and low maintenance as opposed to low installation and high maintenance. The American tradition has become increasingly one of high installation—spending a lot of money putting in utilities that will be inexpensive to maintain and return a high rate of interest on the bonds needed to fund them. Canyon, on the contrary, would have financed and cared for the system within the community.

"Look at that," he says with disgust, holding out his left arm. It is trembling uncontrollably, as though it is being shaken by an unseen hand.

"I thought I had forgotten all that, but it's all come back."

Wearily, as though physically feeling the hundreds of hours of work, the argument, the rejection, he holds his left arm steady with his right hand and looks out over the trees.

"I despair that people, officials particularly, will recognize the need for self-contained systems like this, yet will do nothing to assist the development of alternatives.

"There are plenty of people I know who are still trying to make it in the system, working at good nine-to-five jobs with social concern. They are still within the Machine, and the Machine produces eventual disaster.

"All over the country, young people are trying to work out alternative ways of living. With so many of them trying, so many different ways, there are bound to be some that will succeed, that will make it. I believe, with some optimism, that an alternative style is not only possible, but that it is well under way."

He says that he is preparing to leave for a farm on an island in the Straits of Juan de Fuca, part of British Columbia, where he will work and live communally. He estimates that rural British Columbia has about ten years of grace "before the full onslaught of Machine Civilization."

"What I feel is the best part of society is now opting out. Why don't you do it?"

"I don't think everybody is prepared to live like this, in nature."

He laughs. "You come out of the womb equipped to live in nature. It's possible to do anything that you want to do."

"I wish I could believe that."

We shook hands then, and I wished him luck and said goodbye, and I left him standing bareass in the pine trees.